Introduction
to
.NET Aspire

Cloud-native microservices
development with .NET Aspire

Naga Santhosh Reddy Vootukuri

Tommaso Stocchi

bpb

www.bpbonline.com

First Edition 2025

Copyright © BPB Publications, India

ISBN: 978-93-65893-540

To View Complete
BPB Publications Catalogue
Scan the QR Code:

Dedicated to

My beloved parents and sister
and
My wife, Sandhya, and kids, Sky Reddy and Rio Reddy
- Naga Santhosh Reddy Vootukuri

My beloved partner Chiara, for always believing in me
and
My family, without them, I would not be who I am
- Tommaso Stocchi

Foreword

When Tommaso and Naga Santhosh Reddy told me they were writing a book about Aspire, I was excited and a little nervous for them! Aspire is so much more than a traditional framework, stack, language, tool, etc. It's tools, templates, packages, opinions, and extensible by design. How do you cover that in a book?

After following their journey and seeing the final product, I'm proud to admit that they absolutely nailed it. This book walks you through the core pieces of Aspire, defining your app model, plugging in different tools and systems, and monitoring your stack, with deeper dives into patterns we're seeing customers use today in their production apps.

When talking about Aspire, it's important to remember that I said "patterns", not definitive guides or the "right way" to do something. Aspire was built to fit into your world, not lock you into ours. While we start you off with some opinions on fundamental app building blocks, you can wield Aspire however you like. As you follow these brilliant examples and start applying those learnings to your own stacks, you'll realize just how flexible Aspire is, and it will become your secret weapon. When a new hire is fixing bugs before their first lunch, or you're swapping databases with zero drama, or delivering new features in record time, you'll thank the authors for the tools and inspiration this book gave you.

Aspire is young, just over a year as a stable release at the time of writing, which means it's changing a LOT. Some of these APIs might change, new patterns will emerge, new opportunities with AI, observability, and deployment may be unlocked, but this book sets you up for success regardless. You will learn why Aspire is so powerful for the entire dev lifecycle, and you'll start seeing opportunities everywhere to "Aspireify" away developer toil.

We've seen it happen time and time again, and we're building more ways for you to streamline modern app development every day. Go into this book with an open mind. The opportunities are endless.

I hope you enjoy Aspire as much as I've enjoyed building it.

Maddy Montaquila
Lead Product Manager, Aspire
Microsoft

About the Authors

- **Naga Santhosh Reddy Vootukuri** works for Microsoft as a principal software engineering manager in the Azure SQL product. He has more than 17 years of experience in designing and developing several products within Microsoft, ranging from SSIS to MDS, and currently in Azure SQL DB. He has deep knowledge in cloud computing, distributed systems, AI, microservice-based architecture, and cloud-native apps, and has experience working in three different Microsoft centers (India, China, and the United States). Santhosh has authored and published numerous research articles in peer-reviewed and indexed journals and in major trade publications. He is a core MVB blogger at DZone and an active senior IEEE member handling various conferences as technical chair in the Seattle IEEE region. He also manages several open-source projects on GitHub, which have several stars. He has participated in and judged industry-wide hackathons related to AI, which were widely popular on DevPost. He frequently speaks and presents at various conferences about microservices, AI, and cloud computing. He actively mentors junior engineers on ADPList and contributes widely to the developer community. Naga is in the top 1% of developers in the cloud and AI community. Naga has been awarded the prestigious Docker Captain membership program for his outstanding contributions to the Docker and containers community.

- **Tomasso Stocchi** is a cloud solution architect for Microsoft's application innovation team. He helps developers leverage Microsoft's technologies to build cloud-native intelligent applications and implement DevOps practices. He has extensive experience and knowledge in cloud computing and software development.

About the Reviewers

❖ **Gopal Singh** is a distinguished product engineer at Google, bringing extensive expertise in software development, with a focus on automation and AI.

He is the author of 4 patents and 2 defensive publications, underscoring his innovative contributions to the field.

His technical proficiencies include .NET, C#, Python, **Google Cloud Platform (GCP)**, and **Robotic Process Automation (RPA)**.

❖ **Vahid Farahmandian** is a C# Corner MVP, software architect, and globally recognized technology expert specializing in enterprise-scale .NET solutions, cloud-based systems, and DevOps transformation. A frequent speaker at international tech conferences, he shares insights on software innovation and system design. With a career spanning consulting for multinational enterprises and architecting mission-critical systems, Vahid has authored technical books that shape industry practices.

As the creator of the Jinget framework, widely used to streamline .NET development, he drives technical excellence at Spoota company, leading teams to deliver scalable, high-impact solutions. Passionate about knowledge sharing, Vahid teaches Azure DevOps and modern software architecture, empowering developers to bridge theory and practice.

Acknowledgements

I would like to thank my wife, Sandhya, for supporting me throughout this journey, as it involved countless hours of work over the weekends, and she always encouraged me to pursue my dreams. Grateful to my parents and sister. Thanks to my team (SQL deployment – RDM) and my managers (Mohamed El Hassouni and Brian Chamberlain) at Microsoft, both encouraged and supported me when I told them about my book-writing journey. Finally, lots of love to my kids, Sky and Rio. I also extend my deepest gratitude and thanks to the following people:

Tommaso Stocchi: My partner and fellow author of this book, we live in different countries and different time zones, yet we never had any issues in meeting and discussing the book. I am glad we collaborated on this book and, hopefully, will continue to do so for many more books in the future.

Thanks to the technical reviewers of this book. They played a key role in providing great feedback and suggestions, which helped in improving the book's overall quality. They have thorough knowledge in this area, and I appreciate the hours of work they dedicated to reviewing this book. Thank you, and hopefully, we will collaborate on more books in the future.

Lastly, I would like to thank all the people from the C# and Azure developer community, the broader open-source community, who purchased this book and are reading this page. I hope this book will play a key role in your learning journey of exploring .NET Aspire with a practical example.

My gratitude also goes to the entire team at BPB Publications for being supportive and helping me and Tommaso to release this book.

- Naga Santhosh Reddy Vootukuri

I would like to thank Chiara, my partner, who always supported me in spending all those nights diving into new technologies and learning new skills. She always helped me pursue my dreams.

Thanks to my family, who always supported me in evolving as a person and building the life I have today.

Thanks to Frank Boucher, my dear ex-colleague, who supported and helped me join the open-source Aspire community and connect with the Aspire team. This book would not have been possible without all those insights.

Thanks to Naga Santhosh Reddy Vootukuri (Sunny), my partner and fellow author of this book, who helped me go through this first experience writing a book. Despite living in different countries and different time zones, he has always been available to meet and discuss the book. I am glad we collaborated on this book and, hopefully, will continue to do so for many more books in the future.

Also, I would like to thank the Aspire team, who constantly spend time getting in touch with the communities while innovating to improve the developer experience.

-Tommaso Stocchi

Preface

In recent years, the app development landscape has changed considerably. More organizations are migrating to cloud-native designs, and developers now have the daunting task of building, deploying, and managing these distributed systems. For many developers, this shift will involve a whole host of challenges in terms of putting together a set of technology stacks, managing configuration, service discovery, observability, deployment, and many other best practices. The complexity of the underlying architecture may seem overwhelming as well.

That is where .NET Aspire comes in .NET Aspire can be a term that describes an opinionated, cloud-ready stack for building observable, production-ready, distributed applications. .NET Aspire will introduce a range of topics and capabilities that are common to developers who build applications for the cloud. When we began planning to write a book on .NET Aspire, we were motivated because we experienced (and continue to experience) the challenges of developers building distributed applications (configuration, service discovery, observability, deployment, etc.). This book is a culmination of our experiences with .NET Aspire from its genesis. More than just explaining everything that .NET Aspire has to offer, this book provides examples of what can be achieved using .NET Aspire and explains how and the trade-offs of alternative implementations, should you decide to pursue one or more in your own implementation.

This book takes a practical approach for .NET Aspire learners. It covers a few real-time industry examples as well. This book is divided into 8 chapters. They will cover .NET Aspire basics all the way to implementing a real-world solution, along with deployment and monitoring. We also made sure to accommodate some of the latest feature releases from .NET Aspire 9.3 version (AI). So, learners can get more interest in learning .NET Aspire and also stay current. The details are listed below.

Chapter 1: Introduction to .NET Aspire- This chapter introduces the challenges of distributed application development and the evolution of .NET Aspire from Project Tye. Then explores .NET Aspire capabilities by introducing architecture to build a real-world application throughout this book.

Chapter 2: .NET Aspire Integrations- This chapter covers how .NET Aspire enables seamless integration with databases and external services by demonstrating practical steps to connect .NET services to a database using **data API builder (DAB)**.

Chapter 3: .NET Aspire and Other Languages- This chapter expands your view into a wider world of integrations by demonstrating how to integrate services written in different programming languages (Go, Node.js, Python) alongside .NET components, highlighting service discovery and observability across language boundaries.

Chapter 4: .NET Aspire Monitoring- This chapter discusses monitoring and observability, essential for all production-ready distributed systems, in detail. Introduces OpenTelemetry and demonstrates how to instrument .NET Aspire applications for logs, metrics, and traces, ensuring reliability and performance.

Chapter 5: Deployments Using azd- The chapter looks at deployment strategies that would normally be done with **Azure Developer CLI (azd)**, connecting the development phase to production.

Chapter 6: Integrating with Dapr- This chapter introduces Dapr integration, providing you with high-leverage distributed application characteristics for your .NET Aspire projects. Explains Dapr's building blocks and demonstrates how to leverage service invocation and pub/sub messaging to enhance scalability and resilience.

Chapter 7: .NET Aspire Unit Testing- This chapter takes you through testing strategies and exercises to ensure reliable and maintainable distributed applications. This chapter guides readers through setting up test projects, writing effective tests, and leveraging Aspire's orchestration for end-to-end testing.

Chapter 8: .NET Aspire and AI- This chapter explores how .NET Aspire can be used to build intelligent, AI-driven applications. Introduces large language models, orchestrators, and agents, and demonstrates integration with frameworks like Semantic Kernel and Azure OpenAI.

Code Bundle and Coloured Images

Please follow the link to download the
Code Bundle and the *Coloured Images* of the book:

https://rebrand.ly/791f62

The code bundle for the book is also hosted on GitHub at
https://github.com/bpbpublications/Introduction-to-.Net-Aspire.
In case there's an update to the code, it will be updated on the existing
GitHub repository.

We have code bundles from our rich catalogue of books and videos
available at https://github.com/bpbpublications. Check them out!

Errata

We take immense pride in our work at BPB Publications and follow
best practices to ensure the accuracy of our content to provide with an
indulging reading experience to our subscribers. Our readers are our
mirrors, and we use their inputs to reflect and improve upon human
errors, if any, that may have occurred during the publishing processes
involved. To let us maintain the quality and help us reach out to any
readers who might be having difficulties due to any unforeseen errors,
please write to us at :

errata@bpbonline.com

Your support, suggestions and feedbacks are highly appreciated by the
BPB Publications' Family.

Did you know that BPB offers eBook versions of every book
published, with PDF and ePub files available? You can upgrade
to the eBook version at www.bpbonline.com and as a print book
customer, you are entitled to a discount on the eBook copy. Get in
touch with us at :
business@bpbonline.com for more details.

At www.bpbonline.com, you can also read a collection of free
technical articles, sign up for a range of free newsletters, and
receive exclusive discounts and offers on BPB books and eBooks.

Piracy

If you come across any illegal copies of our works in any form on the internet, we would be grateful if you would provide us with the location address or website name. Please contact us at **business@bpbonline.com** with a link to the material.

If you are interested in becoming an author

If there is a topic that you have expertise in, and you are interested in either writing or contributing to a book, please visit **www.bpbonline.com**. We have worked with thousands of developers and tech professionals, just like you, to help them share their insights with the global tech community. You can make a general application, apply for a specific hot topic that we are recruiting an author for, or submit your own idea.

Reviews

Please leave a review. Once you have read and used this book, why not leave a review on the site that you purchased it from? Potential readers can then see and use your unbiased opinion to make purchase decisions. We at BPB can understand what you think about our products, and our authors can see your feedback on their book. Thank you!

For more information about BPB, please visit **www.bpbonline.com**.

Join our Discord space

Join our Discord workspace for latest updates, offers, tech happenings around the world, new releases, and sessions with the authors:

https://discord.bpbonline.com

Table of Contents

1. Introduction to .NET Aspire 1

    Introduction...1

    Structure..1

    Objectives 2

    Common distributed application struggles............................2

    History of .NET Aspire..2

    .NET Aspire..4

       Solution 5

    .NET Aspire template 6

       Using command line interface 7

       Using Visual Studio 2022 7

    Reference architecture...18

    Conclusion..20

2. .NET Aspire Integrations.. 21

    Introduction...21

    Structure..21

    Objectives 22

    Setting up a development environment 22

    Benefits of .NET Aspire integrations 23

    Understanding .NET Aspire integrations.......................24

    Data API builder...28

    Create warehouse backend API 29

       Using the command line interface...............................29

       Using Visual Studio 2022 30

    Understanding the code structure 33

dab-config.json...33

Warehouseclient.cs 35

launchsettings.json...37

appsettings.json...38

Program configuration 39

Adding data API builder to the AppHost 40

.NET Aspire Community Toolkit..47

Running Eshop Aspire from Visual Studio 47

Use .http files in Visual Studio to validate API..................48

Conclusion..49

3. .NET Aspire and Other Languages.....................................51

Introduction...51

Structure..51

Objectives 52

Setting up a development environment...............................52

Benefits of a polyglot microservices architecture 53

Integrating services with .NET Aspire................................54

Implementing different microservices 54

Orchestrating external services with .NET Aspire 64

Conclusion..73

4. .NET Aspire Monitoring...75

Introduction...75

Structure..75

Objectives 76

Monitoring in cloud-native applications 76

Key benefits of monitoring 76

Observability..77

OpenTelemetry fundamentals..78

Benefits of OpenTelemetry..79

OpenTelemetry components..79

OpenTelemetry instrumentation..80

Instrumenting .NET Aspire applications with
OpenTelemetry 80

Setting up OpenTelemetry inside WarehouseAPI project.....80

Health checks in .NET Aspire..85

Analyzing and visualizing Telemetry 87

Conclusion..91

5. Deployments Using azd.. 93

Introduction..93

Structure 93

Objectives 94

Introduction to azd and its benefits................................94

Installation and configuration of azd 96

Use azd with .NET Aspire..101

Development and deployment of Eshop
application using azd..119

Advanced azd features..130

Conclusion..133

6. Integrating with Dapr 135

Introduction..135

Structure..135

Objectives 136

Distributed Application Runtime 136

Importance of Dapr..138

Getting started with Dapr 139

Using Dapr in .NET Aspire..141

Adding Dapr to the remaining APIs 144

Configuring Dapr for Azure deployment...........................151

Conclusion...153

7. .NET Aspire Testing... 155

Introduction..155

Structure..156

Objectives 156

Importance of testing in distributed systems.....................156

Testing in .NET Aspire..156

Setting up test projects in .NET Aspire 158

Introduction to unit testing...165

Adding unit tests...165

Executing integration or unit tests 173

Conclusion...174

8. .NET Aspire and AI 177

Introduction..177

Structure..177

Objectives 178

Introduction to LLMs and orchestrator...............................178

Using .NET Aspire when building AI applications...........184

Future trends and upcoming releases 195

Conclusion.. 200

Index 201-204

CHAPTER 1
Introduction to .NET Aspire

Introduction

In this chapter, we will discuss challenges and struggles every developer faced during their distributed application development and how .NET product team addressed these challenges with Project Tye. It was a great experiment which aimed to simplify microservices development by running many services with one command. Project Tye lasted for two years and by gathering and incorporating feedback it led to the creation of .NET Aspire. We will explore all the details in the upcoming sections.

Structure

In this chapter, we will discuss the following topics:

- Common distributed application struggles
- History of .NET Aspire
- .NET Aspire

- .NET Aspire template
- Reference architecture

Objectives

By the end of the chapter, you will learn about why we need .NET Aspire and what common problems it will solve in building distributed microservices, create a sample .NET Aspire project using a starter template and understand various details, including monitoring and setup. You will also learn about the reference architecture of a practical Eshop application using a microservices architecture pattern. This knowledge will help you to follow other chapters in this book.

Common distributed application struggles

Writing distributed applications is not an easy task. There are many challenges to face from local development all the way to production.

Think about a very simple distributed application. Let us discuss, we have a frontend displaying some weather forecasts, an API exposing those data, and a cache in which the frontend can save data received from the backend.

Some of the questions that come to mind are:

- What is the API URL?
- What is the cache URL?
- Which port should we use?
- How can I run everything locally?
- How can I deploy my application to production?

If this seems familiar to you, you are not alone. Every developer struggles with these issues, and many have tried to solve them.

History of .NET Aspire

The .NET product group first tried to address these issues with Project Tye. It was the .NET tool with the following clear goals:

- Making the development of microservices easier by:
  - o Running many services with one command.
  - o Using dependencies in containers.
  - o Discovering addresses of other services using simple conventions.
- Automating deployment of .NET applications to Kubernetes by:
  - o Automatically containerizing .NET applications.
  - o Generating Kubernetes manifests with minimal knowledge or configuration.
  - o Using a single configuration file.

Analyzing the goals of this tool, we can clearly see that the aim was simply to find an answer to most of the struggles mentioned above.

Using Project Tye, we could define all the different resources, both projects and containers such as Redis, of our distributed application, and tie them together to run everything locally. It even offered extension packages such as configuration to read certain environment variables where needed.

```
dotnet add frontend/frontend.csproj package Microsoft.Tye.
Extensions.Configuration   --version "0.2.0-*"
...
public void ConfigureServices(IServiceCollection services)
{
    services.AddRazorPages();
    /** Add the following to wire the client to the backend
**/
    services.AddHttpClient<WeatherClient>(client =>
    {
                client.BaseAddress    =    Configuration.
GetServiceUri("backend");
    });
    /** End added code **/
}
...
```

Note: **The above code is an excerpt from `startup.cs` of the frontend project.**

Running our solution using the Tye CLI would result in a dashboard containing all our resources (shown in *Figure 1.1*):

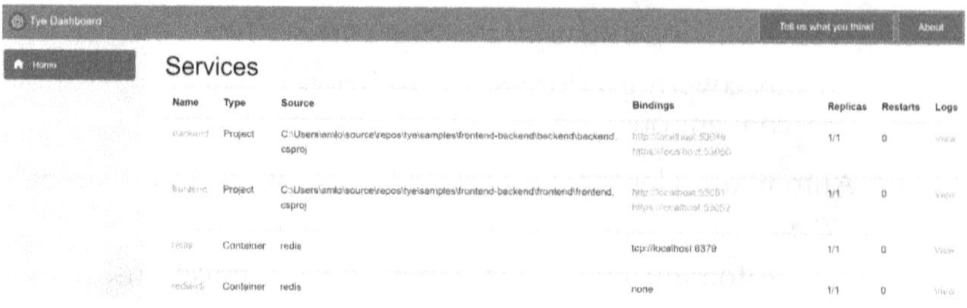

Figure 1.1: *Tye Dashboard with a list of all services*

Detailed relative logs for the frontend application is shown in *Figure 1.2:*

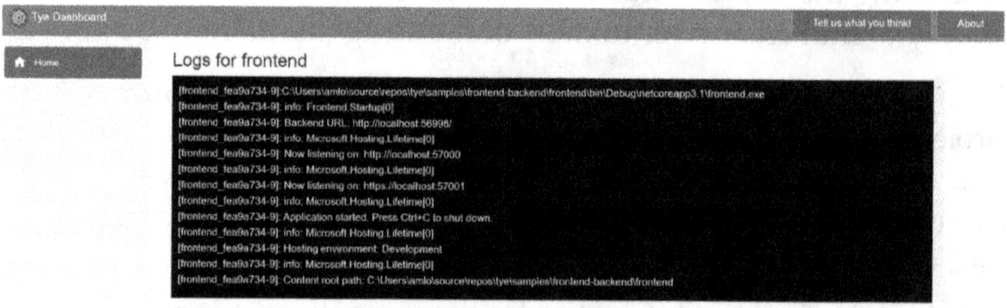

Figure 1.2: *The dashboard with detailed frontend logs*

Project Tye was a great experiment that lasted for about two years. The product group gathered feedback and decided to build and improve upon it, and it led to the creation of .NET Aspire. A lot of concepts coming from Project Tye were kept. Some of the foundational concepts, like running multiple services with one command, using dependencies in containers, and service discovery, are carried forward into .NET Aspire with improvements based on feedback gathered during the developmental phases.

.NET Aspire

.NET Aspire is a cloud-native application stack built on top of .NET. It is designed to simplify the process of development, deployment, and management of cloud-native applications. It offers a comprehensive set of tools and features that help in the overall development lifecycle and improve the performance and reliability of cloud-native applications. Following is the .NET Aspire definition from official

Microsoft Learn documentation:

> *.NET Aspire is an opinionated, cloud ready stack for building observable, production ready, distributed applications.*

> *-.NET Aspire Team*

Let us break down the above sentence word by word to understand it better:

- **Opinionated**: This means .NET Aspire has specific ways of doing things, which it does by providing specific guidelines, best practices, and conventions that it enforces. It provides strong suggestions on how to structure, implement, and maintain the software using the .NET Aspire framework.

- **Cloud-ready**: Cloud-ready or cloud-native applications are mainly designed to work well in cloud environments, such as Azure, AWS, or Google Cloud. It is designed to leverage cloud computing characteristics such as scalability, availability, performance, and security by default.

- **Observable**: These applications are easy to monitor by providing insights into their internal state, behavior, and performance.

- **Production ready**: These applications are ready to be deployed to production environments. They are reliable, scalable, and secure to meet the demands of a production application.

- **Distributed applications**: This refers to applications that run on multiple computers or servers, often spread across different locations and that work together to represent a single system.

Solution

.NET Aspire was mainly created to solve the pain points of distributed application developers, where they face problems in running and debugging multiple cloud native applications on their local development machine. It streamlines configuration management and dependency injection, which helps in setup. .NET Aspire supports distributed tracing to visualize every request flow across microservices, which helps in debugging. .NET Aspire helps with the following:

- **Orchestration**: .NET Aspire provides features for running and connecting multi-project applications and their dependencies for local development environments.

- **Integrations**: .NET Aspire integrations are NuGet packages for commonly used services, such as Redis or Postgres, with standardized interfaces ensuring they connect consistently and seamlessly with your app.

- **Tooling**: .NET Aspire comes with project templates and tooling experiences for Visual Studio and the .NET **command line interface (CLI)**, which help you create and interact with .NET Aspire apps. Integration with popular logging and telemetry frameworks (for example, Serilog and OpenTelemetry) helps in monitoring and troubleshooting.

- **Cloud-native deployment**: .NET Aspire simplifies the deployment and management of cloud-native applications due to seamless integration with container orchestration platforms like Kubernetes.

- **Security**: .NET Aspire's built-in security features and integrations with industry-standard security frameworks help in protecting your data and building resilient cloud-native applications. It enforces HTTPS (secure communication protocol) to prevent data tampering.

.NET Aspire template

.NET Aspire offers a few different templates. These can be divided into templates we can use to start integrating our code with Aspire easily, templates we can use to see common patterns for Aspire, and templates for unit tests. You can list them all by typing the following:

```
dotnet new --list
```

The following is the list of templates available:

- **Integration**:

    o **.NET Aspire app host**: aspire-apphost

    o **.NET Aspire empty app**: aspire

    o **.NET Aspire service defaults**: aspire-servicedefaults

- **Starter templates:**
  - o   **.NET Aspire starter app**: aspire-starter
- **Unit tests:**
  - o   **.NET Aspire test project (MSTest)**: aspire-mstest
  - o   **.NET Aspire test project (NUnit)**: aspire-nunit
  - o   **.NET Aspire test project (xUnit)**: aspire-xunit

The .NET Aspire starter app is the one we are going to look at in this introductory chapter. We can create a new .NET Aspire starter application using either Visual Studio, Visual Studio Code, or the .NET CLI.

Using command line interface

Let us start by opening a new terminal session and running the following commands to create an empty folder and create our starter app:

```
mkdir FirstApp
cd FirstApp
dotnet new aspire-starter
```

We can append the **flag-use-redis-cache** to add Redis integration to our starter app, but we will look at this in future chapters.

Using Visual Studio 2022

At the top of Visual Studio, navigate to **File** | **New** | **Project**. In the dialog window (shown in *Figure 1.3*), search for Aspire and select the **.NET Aspire Starter App** template.

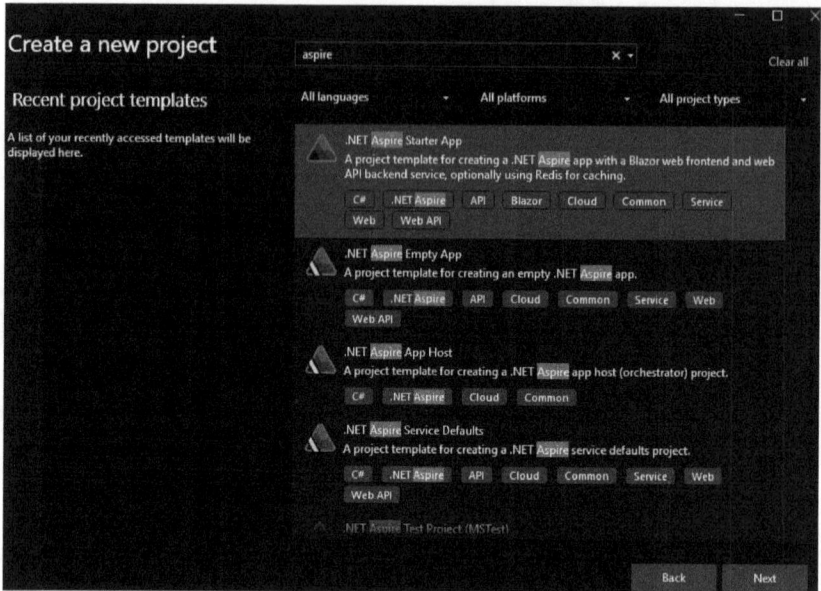

Figure 1.3: *Visual Studio 2022 project template window*

Click **Next** to add the project name and additional information, as shown in *Figure 1.4*:

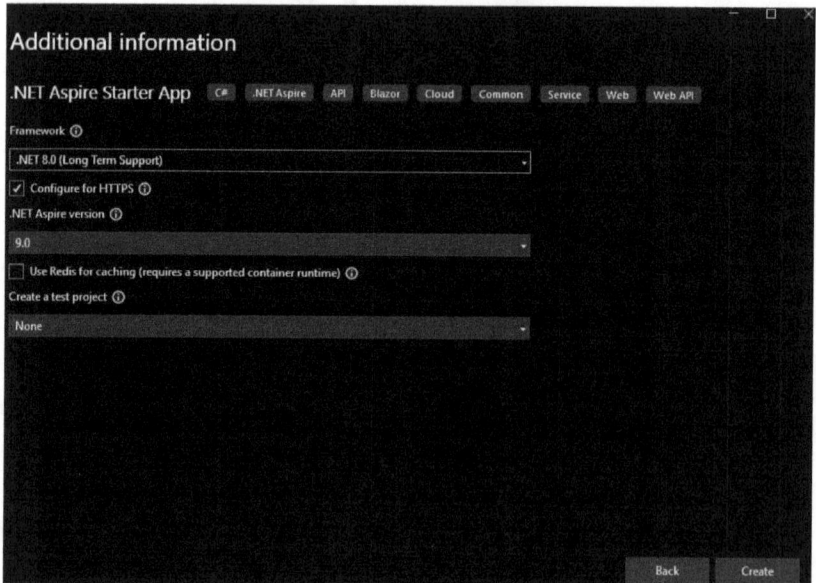

Figure 1.4: *.NET Aspire starter app additional information dialog*

After we open the created solution in our preferred editor, we will see four projects in the **Solution Explorer**, as shown in the following *Figure 1.5*:

- **FirstApp.ApiService**
- **FirstApp.AppHost**
- **FirstApp.ServiceDefaults**
- **FirstApp.Web**

Figure 1.5: *Solution explorer view of newly created application opened from Visual Studio 2022*

If you are familiar with .NET, you might already know both **FirstApp. Web** and **FirstApp.ApiService**. **FirstApp.Web** is the classic Blazor frontend, which reads weather data from **FirstApp.ApiService**, which is a .NET minimal **application programming interface (API)** project that returns random weather forecasts.

Nonetheless, both projects contain some lines of code you might have never seen, and those come from .NET Aspire, specifically from **FirstApp.ServiceDefaults**. This project is the opinionated part of .NET Aspire, a collection of extension methods that implement a series of best practices.

Let us break this project down into all the different methods:

```
public static TBuilder AddServiceDefaults<TBuilder>(this
TBuilder builder) where TBuilder : IHostApplicationBuilder
    {
        builder.ConfigureOpenTelemetry();

        builder.AddDefaultHealthChecks();

        builder.Services.AddServiceDiscovery();
        builder.Services.ConfigureHttpClientDefaults(http =>
```

```
    {
        // Turn on resilience by default
        http.AddStandardResilienceHandler();

        // Turn on service discovery by default
        http.AddServiceDiscovery();
    });

    // Uncomment the following to restrict the allowed
schemes for service discovery.
                            //      builder.Services.
Configure<ServiceDiscoveryOptions>(options =>
        // {
        //      options.AllowedSchemes = ["https"];
        // });

    return builder;
}
```

AddServiceDefaults, as can be deduced by the name, adds default services to the **ApplicationBuilder** that invokes it. Such services are as follows:

- Telemetry

- HealthChecks

- ServiceDiscovery

- Default configuration for HttpClient

You might notice that the code to restrict allowed schemes to HTTPS only is commented on. This is because that is a setting that cannot always be applied but should be when possible. This is the reason why the ServiceDefaults project is not a NuGet package, but a project, so that the developer can freely extend it and adapt it to its needs.

Another example of this can be found in the **ConfigureOpenTelemetry** method and in the **AddOpenTelemetryExporters**, where the developer can choose whether to enable **GrpcClientInstrumentation** on top of **HttpClientInstrumentation** and to add other exporters on top of the default one (provided by .NET Aspire itself).

The other useful method we can find is **MapDefaultEndoints** are as follows:

```
    public static WebApplication MapDefaultEndpoints(this
WebApplication app)
    {
        // Adding health checks endpoints to applications
in non-development environments has security implications.
        // See https://aka.ms/dotnet/aspire/healthchecks for
details before enabling these endpoints in non-development
environments.
        if (app.Environment.IsDevelopment())
        {
            // All health checks must pass for app to be
considered ready to accept traffic after starting
            app.MapHealthChecks("/health");

            // Only health checks tagged with the "live"
tag must pass for app to be considered alive
        app.MapHealthChecks("/alive", new HealthCheckOptions
            {
                Predicate = r => r.Tags.Contains("live")
            });
        }

        return app;
    }
```

This method is used to extend the **WebApplication** object, as it maps standard health checks and live endpoints.

Having these methods in the ServiceDefaults project is not enough. We need to invoke them where needed, starting with the **Program. cs** of **FirstApp.ApiService**, we can see where these are used:

```
var builder = WebApplication.CreateBuilder(args);

// Add service defaults & Aspire client integrations.
builder.AddServiceDefaults();

// Add services to the container.
```

```
builder.Services.AddProblemDetails();


// Learn more about configuring OpenAPI at https://aka.ms/
aspnet/openapi
builder.Services.AddOpenApi();
...
app.MapGet("/weatherforecast", () =>
{
    var forecast = Enumerable.Range(1, 5).Select(index =>
        new WeatherForecast
        (
        DateOnly.FromDateTime(DateTime.Now.AddDays(index)),
            Random.Shared.Next(-20, 55),
            summaries[Random.Shared.Next(summaries.Length)]
        ))
        .ToArray();
    return forecast;
})
.WithName("GetWeatherForecast");


app.MapDefaultEndpoints();


app.Run();
```

The same happens in the **Program.cs** of the **FirstApp.Web** project. In the **Program.cs** of the frontend project, we can also see the first benefits of using .NET Aspire, if we take a look at how the HttpClient for the API is created:

```
builder.Services.AddHttpClient<WeatherApiClient>(client
=>
    {
        // This URL uses "https+http://" to indicate HTTPS
is preferred over HTTP.
        // Learn more about service discovery scheme
resolution at https://aka.ms/dotnet/sdschemes.
        client.BaseAddress = new("https+http://apiservice");
    });
```

As you can see, there are no endpoints, no localhost, and no specified port. Only the string **https+http://apiservice.** How can this work? This is not something we can only achieve via .NET Aspire. Service discovery is supported by .NET if properly configured, and that is what .NET Aspire has done for us via the **AddServiceDefaults** method.

.NET has the capability, once the service discovery has been configured, to retrieve the endpoints and connection strings for certain resources from the **appsettings.json** file:

```
"Logging": {
    "LogLevel": {
      "Default": "Information",
      "Microsoft.AspNetCore": "Warning"
    }
  },
  "Services": {
    "apiservice": {
      "https": [
        "https://localhost:44300"
      ]
  },
  "AllowedHosts": "*"
```

Having a configuration such as this one in the **appsettings.json** file would allow us to add an HttpClient for our **apiservice**, as we did above. If you look at the **appsettings.json** of the FirstApp.Web project, you will find nothing similar. How can this work, then?

Well, when we run the **FirstApp.AppHost** project, we will see that .NET Aspire injects the correct URL of the **apiservice** as an environment variable of the frontend. It will use the format **services__apiservice__http__0**. This linear format for the environment variable maps the entire structure of the json. The 0, in the end, is necessary since the accepted value for the **http** field is an array.

Since we have **https+http** in the URL of the **apiservice** at the code level, .NET service discovery will prefer the use of an HTTP endpoint if available.

As the final step, let us look at the **FirstApp.AppHost** project. This one is the entrypoint of our application and contains a **Program.cs** as follows:

```
var builder = DistributedApplication.CreateBuilder(args);

var apiService = builder.AddProject<Projects.FirstApp_
ApiService>("apiservice");

builder.AddProject<Projects.FirstApp_Web>("webfrontend")
    .WithExternalHttpEndpoints()
    .WithReference(apiService)
    .WaitFor(apiService);

builder.Build().Run();
```

The structure is very similar to every other .NET application. As such, we have a builder. In this case, we are building a **DistributedApplication**. We are adding two projects to our builder, using static classes that .NET Aspire has created for us to describe our projects. We can explore the **FirstApp_ApiService** as follows:

```
namespace Projects;

[global::System.CodeDom.Compiler.GeneratedCode("Aspire.
Hosting", null)]
[global::System.Diagnostics.CodeAnalysis.
ExcludeFromCodeCoverage(Justification = "Generated code.")]
[global::System.Diagnostics.DebuggerDisplay("Type        =
{GetType().Name,nq}, ProjectPath = {ProjectPath}")]
public class FirstApp_ApiService : global::Aspire.Hosting.
IProjectMetadata
{
        public string ProjectPath => """D:\src\FirstApp\
FirstApp.ApiService\FirstApp.ApiService.csproj""";
}
```

Besides a few attributes used by the compiler, this class exposes the local path of the project. It is generated for us and will change every time. This is way better than having a local hardcoded path.

Back to the **Program.cs** of the AppHost, we can see that, since the **webfrontend** resource needs access to the **apiservice**, we can simply assign the **ProjectResource** to a variable and then use the **WithReference** method. This will make .NET Aspire inject the **services__apiservice__http__0** environment variable in the **webfrontend** resource at runtime.

The **WaitFor** method allows .NET Aspire to wait for the API service to be healthy before starting the **webfrontend**.

If we run the **Program.cs** of the AppHost project, our browser will open with this dashboard, showing all our resources running as shown in *Figure 1.6*:

Figure 1.6: *.NET Aspire dashboard resources view*

The ports on your machine might (and most likely will) be different. This is because of .NET Aspire and .NET service discovery, we do not have to hardcode any endpoint anymore.

By clicking on the **webfrontend**, line we can explore all the environment variables and configuration for our resource as shown in *Figure 1.7*:

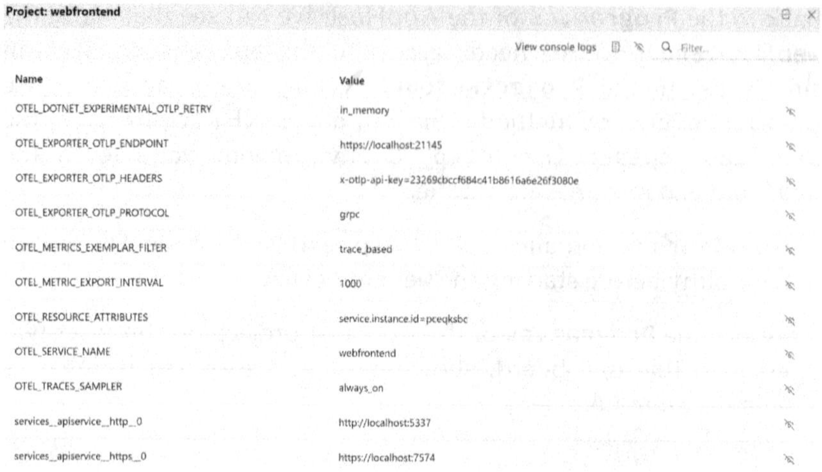

Name	Value	
OTEL_DOTNET_EXPERIMENTAL_OTLP_RETRY	in_memory	
OTEL_EXPORTER_OTLP_ENDPOINT	https://localhost:21145	
OTEL_EXPORTER_OTLP_HEADERS	x-otlp-api-key=23269cbccf684c41b8616a6e26f3080e	
OTEL_EXPORTER_OTLP_PROTOCOL	grpc	
OTEL_METRICS_EXEMPLAR_FILTER	trace_based	
OTEL_METRIC_EXPORT_INTERVAL	1000	
OTEL_RESOURCE_ATTRIBUTES	service.instance.id=pceqksbc	
OTEL_SERVICE_NAME	webfrontend	
OTEL_TRACES_SAMPLER	always_on	
services__apiservice__http__0	http://localhost:5337	
services__apiservice__https__0	https://localhost:7574	

Figure 1.7: webfrontend environment variables view

Note: **We have both HTTP and HTTPS endpoints for the apiservice, and an OpenTelemetry endpoint.**

You will notice that, on the left, we have structured logs, traces, and metrics. Our resources have been instrumented by the ServiceDefaults, and .NET Aspire already provides us with both an OpenTelemetry endpoint and the dashboards to see the metrics.

If we generate some traffic navigating the frontend, we can then explore our traces, as shown in *Figure 1.8*:

Figure 1.8: webfrontend traces view

By clicking on the **GET /weather** call that involves both webfrontend and API service, we can explore all the networking traces, as shown in *Figure 1.9*:

webfrontend: GET /weather

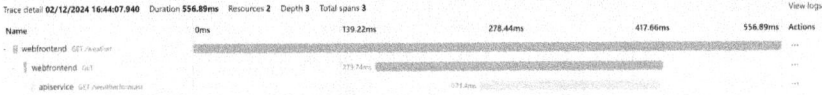

Trace detail 02/12/2024 16:44:07.940 Duration **556.89ms** Resources 2 Depth 3 Total spans **3**   View logs

Name	0ms	139.22ms	278.44ms	417.66ms	556.89ms	Actions
webfrontend GET /weather						...
webfrontend Get	273.74ms					...
apiservice GET /weatherforecast		071.4ms				...

Figure 1.9: Individual web request traces from start to end

By clicking on the **View logs** link in the top right corner, we can explore the **Structured logs** relative to this trace id, as shown in *Figure 1.10*:

Structured logs

Resource (All)   Q Filter...   Level (All)   Filters   TraceId == f8c10bc7cfedcc05747a993079306e08

Resource	Level	Timestamp	Message	Trace	Actions
webfrontend	Information	16:44:08.032	Start processing HTTP request GET https=http://apiservice/weatherforecast	f8c10bc	...
webfrontend	Information	16:44:08.111	Sending HTTP request GET https://localhost:7574/weatherforecast	f8c10bc	...
webfrontend	Information	16:44:08.419	Received HTTP response headers after 278.3592ms - 200	f8c10bc	...
webfrontend	Information	16:44:08.437	Execution attempt. Source: '-standard//Standard-Retry', Operation Key: '', Result: '200', Handle...	f8c10bc	...
webfrontend	Information	16:44:08.449	End processing HTTP request after 421.904ms - 200	f8c10bc	...

Figure 1.10: Structured logs view for a given trace id

In the console tab on the left, we can explore live logs coming from all our running resources, and lastly, we have the metrics as shown in *Figure 1.11*:

Metrics

Resource webfrontend   Last 5 min

- Microsoft.AspNetCore.Hosting
  - http.server.active_requests
  - http.server.request.duration
- Microsoft.AspNetCore.Http.Connections
  - signalr.server.active_connections
- Microsoft.AspNetCore.Routing
  - aspnetcore.routing.match_attempts
- Microsoft.AspNetCore.Server.Kestrel
  - kestrel.active_connections
  - kestrel.active_tls_handshakes
  - kestrel.connection.duration
  - kestrel.queued_connections
  - kestrel.queued_requests
  - kestrel.tls_handshake.duration
- OpenTelemetry.Instrumentation.Runtime
  - process.runtime.dotnet.assemblies.c
  - process.runtime.dotnet.exceptions.c
  - process.runtime.dotnet.gc.allocation
  - process.runtime.dotnet.gc.collection

http.server.request.duration
Duration of HTTP server requests.

Graph Table

0.5
0.4
0.3
0.2
0.1
0
     16:44:00   16:45:00   16:46:00   16:47:00

P50 Seconds   P90 Seconds   P99 Seconds   ● Exemplars

Filters

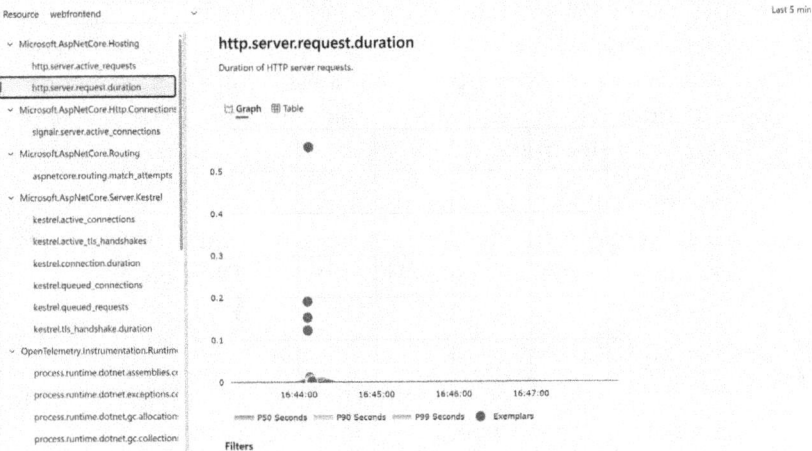

Figure 1.11: webfrontend metrics view with durations and graphs

Reference architecture

This book offers a hands-on, practical application built using a microservices architecture pattern. The application centers around an Eshop application, enabling users to submit orders and receive shipments.

The figure in the following shows the architecture of the solution that we will build throughout the book's chapters (refer to *Figure 1.12*).

The main components of the solution are as follows:

- Web application UI (frontend) developed using React. The user interface allows customers to browse different products, create orders, and view order statuses. The front end communicates with backend services to fetch and update product information in real-time.

- Warehouse API (backend), developed using .NET, handles inventory management. When a request is made to the warehouse API, it will read the warehouse status from the warehouse and the current pending orders from the order database. It will make sure to remove items coming from the pending orders from the available stock in the warehouse.

- Create order API (backend), developed using Golang. When a request is made to the create order API, it will create a new order in the order database and set it to pending. Additionally, it publishes messages to a pub/sub messaging system, initiating the order processing pipeline.

- Payment API (backend) developed using Python. It listens for events from the pub/sub system, and when a request is made to the payment API, it will set the order status to processing.

- Shipping API (backend) developed using Node.js. Once an order is marked as paid, this service is responsible for preparing the shipment, and it will update the status to be completed in the orders database.

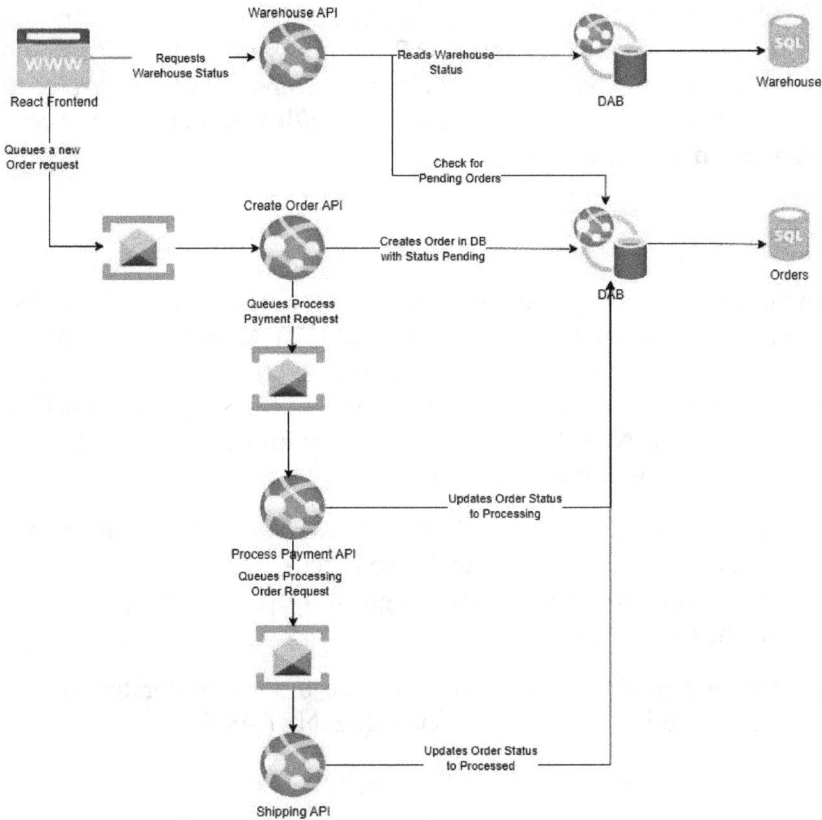

Figure 1.12: *Architecture diagram of an e-commerce application*

The order processing queue implemented using create order API, payment API, and shipping API is implemented using a pub/sub architecture leveraging Redis cache in local development and Azure Service Bus during the deployment.

There are two databases used in this application. They are as follows:

- **Warehouse database**: SQL holds the data for the warehouse.

- **Order database**: SQL holds the order history for pending, processing, and completed orders.

The data layer for the databases is implemented using **data API builder** (**DAB**). DAB provides modern **Representational State Transfer** (**REST**) and GraphQL endpoints to your databases, and it supports both relational and NoSQL. DAB is mainly designed for developers. DAB is cross-platform, open-source and independent of language and frameworks. DAB requires zero code and a single configuration file. For more details on learning about DAB, refer to Microsoft's official documentation **https://learn.microsoft.com/en-us/azure/data-api-builder/**.

Conclusion

In this chapter, we explored problems developers face with distributed applications running locally, introduced .NET Aspire, and explained how it solves the problem. We also introduced the .NET Aspire starter templates to get started. Additionally, we set the stage for a practical exploration of .NET Aspire capabilities by introducing architecture to build a real-world application.

In the next chapter, we will discuss .NET Aspire manifest and monitoring capabilities. We will also discuss .NET Aspire features and build an application from the ground up, providing hands-on experience in the upcoming chapters.

By the end of this book, you will have a solid understanding of building cloud-native applications using .NET Aspire.

Join our Discord space

Join our Discord workspace for latest updates, offers, tech happenings around the world, new releases, and sessions with the authors:

https://discord.bpbonline.com

CHAPTER 2
.NET Aspire Integrations

Introduction

In *Chapter 1, Introduction to .NET Aspire*, we laid out the foundation for the e-commerce application we will be building. Refer to *Chapter 1, Introduction to .NET Aspire*, for details about the application architecture diagram. In this chapter, you will be introduced to the concepts of *.NET Aspire Integrations* and how it is used for creating our first API (warehouse) written in the .NET language. This API will serve as a main component for managing inventory. Another key component, **data API builder (DAB)**, will be introduced. DAB is a tool that automatically generates REST and GraphQL endpoints directly from your database schema, significantly reducing boilerplate code from CRUD operations.

Structure

In this chapter, we will discuss the following topics:

- Setting up a development environment

- Benefits of .NET Aspire integrations
- Understanding .NET Aspire integrations
- Data API builder
- Create warehouse backend API
- Understanding the code structure
- Adding data API builder to the AppHost
- .NET Aspire Community Toolkit
- Running Eshop Aspire from Visual Studio
- Using .http files in Visual Studio to validate API

Objectives

By the end of the chapter, you will gain a comprehensive understanding of .NET Aspire integrations and their practical usage in building distributed applications. You will get familiarized with DAB, which is instrumental in managing database interactions. You will be able to create a functional warehouse API using the .NET language and be able to test it using HTTP files.

Let us look into some prerequisites before we begin.

Setting up a development environment

Make sure you have your development environment set up and configured by installing or setting up the following resources:

- An Azure account with an active subscription **https:// azure.microsoft.com/free/?ref=microsoft.com&utm_ source=microsoft.com&utm_medium=docs&utm_ campaign=visualstudio**

- Dotnet 9.0 or a higher version **https://dotnet.microsoft.com/ en-us/download**

- .NET Aspire SDK **https://learn.microsoft.com/en-us/dotnet/ aspire/fundamentals/dotnet-aspire-sdk**

- PowerShell 7.0 or higher version (For Windows Users only!) **https://learn.microsoft.com/en-us/ powershell/scripting/install/installing-powershell-on-windows?view=powershell-7.4#installing-the-msi-package**

- Install DAB **https://learn.microsoft.com/en-us/azure/data-api-builder/**

- Docker Desktop **https://docs.docker.com/desktop/install/ windows-install/**

- Visual Studio Code **https://code.visualstudio.com/** (or) **Visual studio 2022 - https://visualstudio.microsoft.com/vs/**

- VS Code Docker extension **https://marketplace.visualstudio. com/items?itemName=ms-azuretools.vscode-docker**

- Azure CLI **https://docs.microsoft.com/cli/azure/install-azure-cli**

- Git CLI **https://git-scm.com/**

Note: **At the time of writing this book, we used .NET Aspire 9.2 version throughout the book. However, we covered few important features released in .NET Aspire 9.3 release towards the end of Chapter 8, .NET Aspire and AI.**

Benefits of .NET Aspire integrations

When we are dealing with distributed or cloud-native applications, we do not only have to think about the code itself. If we think about an easy distributed application, we might think of something like a frontend requesting data from a backend. Even in such a simple scenario, it is likely that the frontend will have a cache to store data to prevent invoking the backend too many times. Another example could be having a queue to handle calls between different backend services.

This common pattern led the .NET Aspire team to think about integrations. These are ways of hosting and using common resources such as caches and queues in our .NET Aspire application. .NET

Aspire's NuGet packages are designed to work cohesively, and it helps developers to focus on their application logic rather than spending time dealing with infrastructure complexities.

Understanding .NET Aspire integrations

Firstly, there are two types of integrations: hosting and client resources. **Hosting** resources will actually start a local instance of a certain resource, like a SQL server or a Redis cache. **Client** resources will facilitate the use of a certain resource inside your application, wiring up client libraries to dependency injection. Not all integrations belong to both categories. For instance, there is an integration for OpenAI, but it will not start a local instance of OpenAI. It will let you configure a connection string to an existing OpenAI resource and configure the client to be used inside your code.

To better understand the differences between these two types of Integration, we will consider Redis. This is a scenario in which we have both a hosting and a client resource.

In the previous chapter, we have already seen the aspire-starter template. We can now study the same template, invoking it with the flag **--use-redis-cache**. Firstly, open the command line inside the folder where you want your solution to live, and type:

```
Dotnet new aspire-starter --use-redis-cache
```

This command will create a template with the same projects as the one we have already analyzed. The main differences can be seen inside the **AppHost** and the web projects.

In the **AppHost.csproj** file, we can see that there is a reference to the package **Aspire.Hosting.Redis**:

```
<PackageReference Include="Aspire.Hosting.Redis" Version="9.0.0" />
```

This is the hosting integration, as suggested by the **Hosting** in the package name. In the **Web.csproj** file, we can find the reference to **Aspire.StackExchange.Redis.OutputCaching**:

```
<PackageReference Include="Aspire.StackExchange.Redis.OutputCaching" Version="9.0.0" />
```

This is the .NET Aspire client integration for Redis. The first takeaway from this template is that even when we are dealing with an integration that handles both hosting and client, we need to add two different packages according to the integration type.

If we open the **Program.cs** in the **AppHost** project, we can see the code for the hosting integration:

```
var builder = DistributedApplication.CreateBuilder(args);

var cache = builder.AddRedis("cache");

var apiService = builder.AddProject<Projects.Demo1_
ApiService>("apiservice");

builder.AddProject<Projects.Demo1_Web>("webfrontend")
    .WithExternalHttpEndpoints()
    .WithReference(cache)
    .WaitFor(cache)
    .WithReference(apiService)
    .WaitFor(apiService);

builder.Build().Run();
```

The line we are interested in is:

```
var cache = builder.AddRedis("cache");
```

Here, we add a Redis cache that we call **cache**. The resource name has the same function as the resource names for the **application programming interface (API)** service and the frontend: we can use it to reference the resource using the service discovery.

We can now open the **Program.cs** in the **Web** project to see how we leverage the Redis client integration:

```
using Demo1.Web;
using Demo1.Web.Components;

var builder = WebApplication.CreateBuilder(args);

// Add service defaults & Aspire client integrations.
builder.AddServiceDefaults();
builder.AddRedisOutputCache("cache");
```

```
// Add services to the container.
builder.Services.AddRazorComponents()
    .AddInteractiveServerComponents();

builder.Services.AddHttpClient<WeatherApiClient>(client
=>
    {
        // This URL uses "https+http://" to indicate
HTTPS is preferred over HTTP.
        // Learn more about service discovery scheme
resolution at https://aka.ms/dotnet/sdschemes.
        client.BaseAddress = new("https+http://
apiservice");
    });

var app = builder.Build();

if (!app.Environment.IsDevelopment())
{
    app.UseExceptionHandler("/Error",
createScopeForErrors: true);
    // The default HSTS value is 30 days. You may want to
change this for production scenarios, see https://aka.ms/
aspnetcore-hsts.
    app.UseHsts();
}

app.UseHttpsRedirection();

app.UseAntiforgery();

app.UseOutputCache();

app.MapStaticAssets();

app.MapRazorComponents<App>()
    .AddInteractiveServerRenderMode();

app.MapDefaultEndpoints();

app.Run();
```

At the eighth line, we find:

```
builder.AddRedisOutputCache("cache");
```

This is how we reference the Redis cache named **cache** that we have defined in the **AppHost**.

Running the project can help us better understand what is happening under the hood. If we run the project without a container engine running on our machine, we will see the **cache** resource as unhealthy. Starting the container engine will cause the state to turn to **Running**. This is what the .NET Aspire dashboard should look like, as shown in *Figure 2.1*:

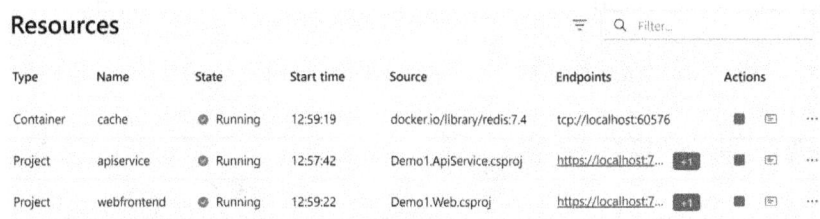

Resources

Type	Name	State	Start time	Source	Endpoints	Actions
Container	cache	⊘ Running	12:59:19	docker.io/library/redis:7.4	tcp://localhost:60576	■ ▣ …
Project	apiservice	⊘ Running	12:57:42	Demo1.ApiService.csproj	https://localhost:7... ＋1	■ ▣ …
Project	webfrontend	⊘ Running	12:59:22	Demo1.Web.csproj	https://localhost:7... ＋1	■ ▣ …

Figure 2.1: .NET dashboard with resources view

Note: **In the Type column, we now have a Container resource, which is our Redis cache. We can also find the running container launching the command in a terminal docker ps.**

Similarly to what happens with the environment variables injection for the **Project** resources, we can see in the following *Figure 2.2* that there is an environment variable for the newly created Redis Cache inside the **webfrontend** project resource:

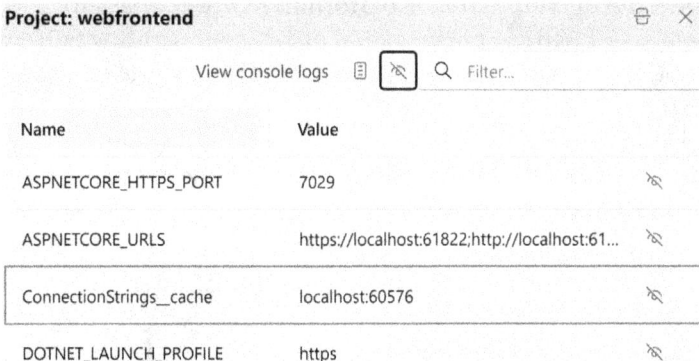

Project: webfrontend

View console logs

Name	Value	
ASPNETCORE_HTTPS_PORT	7029	⊠
ASPNETCORE_URLS	https://localhost:61822;http://localhost:61...	⊠
ConnectionStrings__cache	localhost:60576	⊠
DOTNET_LAUNCH_PROFILE	https	⊠

Figure 2.2: Connection string environment variable details for webfrontend application

Note: Notice how .NET Aspire automatically injects the connection string for the cache (Redis) resource into webfrontend project.

There are many different .NET Aspire integrations, varying from databases (for example, SQL and PostgresDB) to caches (for example, Redis) to cloud resources (for example, Azure Service Bus and OpenAI). It would be an impossible task to describe all of them in a single book, but we will be using a few of them in our architecture to demonstrate the benefits of using them. We advise you to delve into the documentation to discover all the available integrations.

Now that we have a general understanding of what a .NET integration is, we can start building our application from the data side using DAB. After that, we will be able to add DAB as a container to our AppHost and then leverage the integrations to simplify our code.

Data API builder

Data is always at the core of any modern application development. Over this period of time, we have seen many different methods and tools to help developers connect the business layer to the databases. Oftentimes, developers write the same piece of code to perform **create, read, update, delete (CRUD)** operations. DAB was created to help developers with a flexible and powerful framework to rapidly generate APIs that help in bridging the gap between the application layer and the database.

DAB is an open-source (licensed under **Massachusetts Institute of Technology (MIT)**, cross-platform framework where you can spin up modern API endpoints for performing CRUD operations against any database. DAB supports several databases including SQL Server, Azure SQL, Azure Cosmos DB for NoSQL, PostgreSQL, etc. DAB supports both REST and GraphQL endpoints, and it can be executed on-premises or in a container. For more details about DAB, please refer to Microsoft's official documentation **https://learn.microsoft. com/en-us/azure/data-api-builder/overview** . Since it is an open source, anyone interested can contribute by looking at their open issues **https://github.com/azure/data-api-builder/labels/known-issue**

For installing DAB's command line:

```
dotnet tool install microsoft.dataapibuilder –global
```

In DAB, the configuration file is the backbone of its operation. The configuration file is a powerful, flexible tool that helps developers to build robust API's. It is declarative in nature, which not only reduces development time but also ensures consistency and scalability in API management.

The init command is used to generate a new configuration file named **dab-config.json**. It contains details about the database type (for example, MSSQL, SQLServer, Cosmos DB), the connection string, which endpoint to choose (GraphQL/REST or both), and authentication details:

```
dab init
```

To validate the configuration file, run the following command, which checks for syntax errors and makes sure all required fields are populated:

```
dab validate dab-config.json
```

Create warehouse backend API

Once you have a development environment up and running, it is time for us to create the first API backend service (Warehouse API).

You can use Visual Studio or **command line interface** (**CLI**) to create and initialize the .NET Aspire project with Warehouse API.

Using the command line interface

Let us start by opening a new terminal session and running the following commands to create an empty folder and create our starter app:

```
mkdir Eshop
cd Eshop
dotnet new Aspire.AppHost -n Eshop.AppHost
```

We can append flags to add integrations, but for this chapter, it is not needed.

Using Visual Studio 2022

At the top of the Visual Studio, navigate to **File** | **New** | **Project**. In the dialog window (shown in *Figure 2.3*), search for Aspire and select the **.NET Aspire Empty App** template:

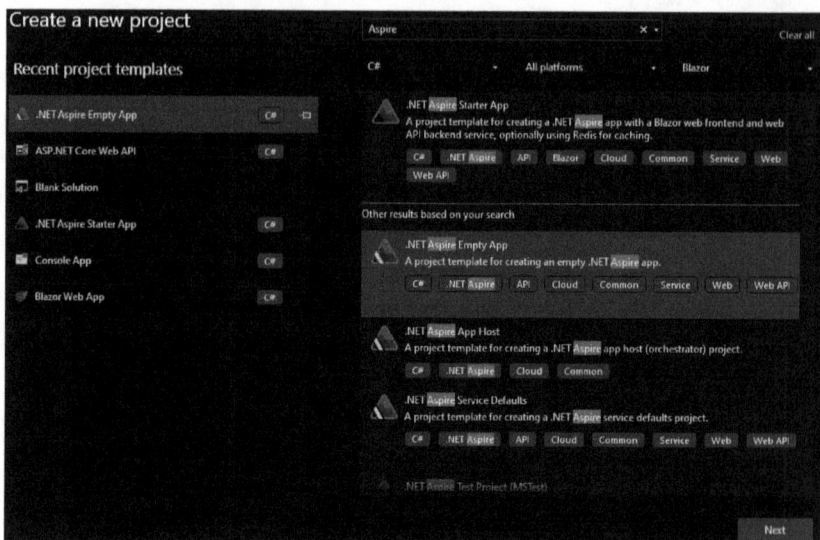

Figure 2.3: *Visual Studio 2022 project template window*

Click **Next** to add the project name and additional information, as shown in *Figure 2.4*:

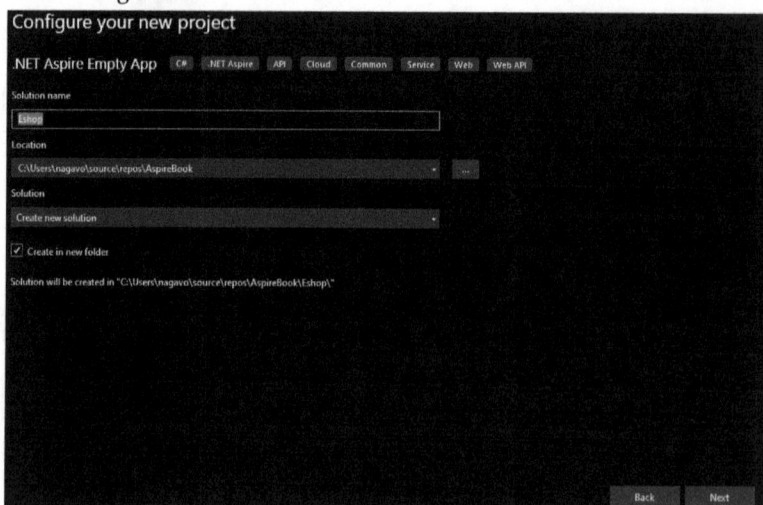

Figure 2.4: *.NET Aspire empty app additional information dialog*

Click **Next** to choose **Framework** as .NET 9.0, as shown in *Figure 2.5:*

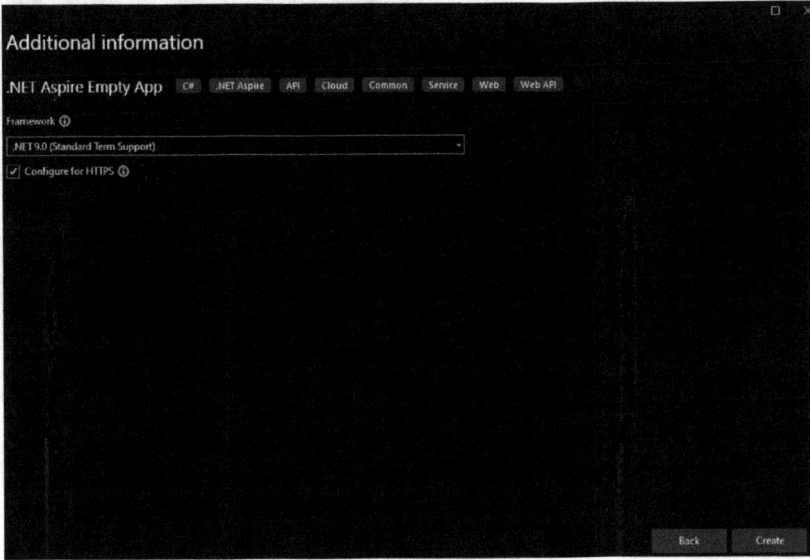

Figure 2.5: .NET Aspire empty app framework selection dialog

After we open the created solution in our preferred editor, we will see two projects in the solution explorer:

- Eshop.AppHost

- Eshop.ServiceDefaults

Let us add the **ASP.NET Core Web API** project, right-click on the solution to select **Add a new project** and search for **web API** in the templates page as shown in *Figure 2.6*:

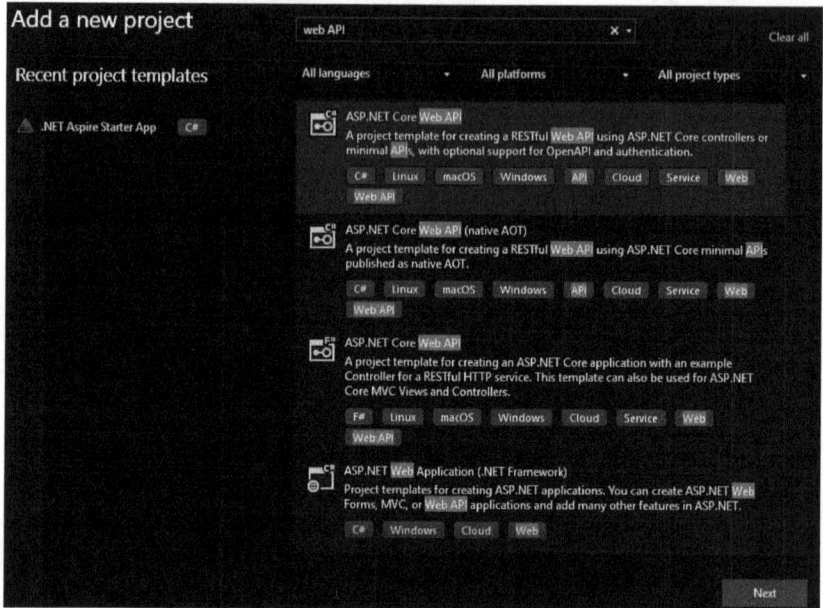

Figure 2.6: Visual Studio template view displaying search results

Click **Next** to enter the project name as WarehouseAPI and location. Click **Next** to enter additional details, as shown in *Figure 2.7*, to create it as a minimal API without controllers:

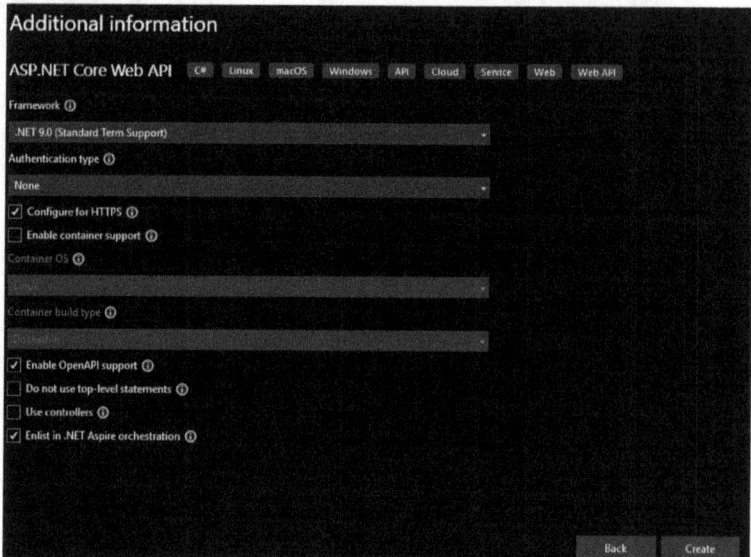

Figure 2.7: ASP.NET Core Web API additional information dialog

Note: **We are creating a minimal API, so we uncheck Use controller, and we check Enable OpenAPI support, so that OpenAPI will help us document and test our API.**

We will now see three projects in the Visual Studio **Solution Explorer** pane, as shown in *Figure 2.8:*

- **Eshop.AppHost**

- **Eshop.ServiceDefaults**

- **WarehouseAPI**

Figure 2.8: Solution Explorer view of the newly created application opened from Visual Studio 2022

Understanding the code structure

Let us take a look at some of the important files within this project to discuss further.

dab-config.json

Create a **dab** folder in the root folder and run **dab init** from cmd line to generate the **dab-config.json** file. Update the file as shown in the following for creating API endpoints for both **WarehouseItems** and **Orders** tables inside **WarehouseDB**. In this chapter, we specified anonymous permissions, which will be updated in the future chapters of this book:

```
{
    "data-source": {
      "database-type": "mssql",
      "connection-string": "@env('ConnectionStrings__
WarehouseDB')"
    },
    "runtime": {
```

```json
    "rest": {
      "path": "/api"
    },
    "graphql": {
      "path": "/graphql"
    },
    "host": {
      "cors": {
        "origins": [],
        "allow-credentials": false
      },
      "mode": "development"
    }
  },
  "entities": {
    "WarehouseItems": {
      "source": "WarehouseItems",
      "permissions": [
        {
          "role": "anonymous",
          "actions": [
            "create",
            "read",
            "update",
            "delete"
          ]
        }
      ],
      "rest": {
        "path": "WarehouseItems"
      }
    },
    "Orders": {
      "source": "Orders",
      "permissions": [
        {
          "role": "anonymous",
          "actions": [
            "create",
            "read",
            "update",
```

```
          "delete"
        ]
      }
    ],
    "rest": {
      "path": "Orders"
    }
  }
}
}
```

Some of the key sections in the above JSON file are:

a. **data-source**: This section defines the database connection type and connection string. In this case, it specifies that the database type is **mssql** and the connection string has an environment placeholder which aspire will substitute during runtime

b. **runtime**: This section outlines the runtime configuration for the API. It includes paths for REST (**/api**) and GrapQL (**/ graphql**) endpoints, as well as host settings such as **cross-origin resource sharing** (**CORS**) configurations and the mode is set to development.

c. **entities**: This section defines the entities that the API will interact with. For example, **WarehouseItems** and **Orders** are specified as sources, with permissions for anonymous roles to perform actions like CRUD. Each entity also has a REST path defined for accessing them.

Warehouseclient.cs

The **Warehouseclient.cs** is designed to interact with Web API to fetch warehouse items and filter out the items that are associated with pending orders. It uses **HttpClient** to make HTTP requests and processes the responses to return the relevant warehouse items. The records define the **Data Transfer Objects** (**DTO**) used in the API responses.

- **DABResponse**: A generic record that represents a response from the DAB. It contains a list of items of type **T**.

- **WarehouseItem**: A record that represents a Warehouse item with properties such as `ItemID, ItemName, Stock` and `LastUpdated`.

- **Order**: A record that represents an order with properties such as `OrderID, CustomerName, ItemID, Quantity, Status, OrderDate` and `LastUpdated`.

```
using System.Linq;

namespace WarehouseAPI;

public class WarehouseClient(HttpClient httpClient)
{
    public async Task<WarehouseItem[]>
GetWarehouseStatus(CancellationToken
cancellationToken = default)
    {
        List<WarehouseItem> items = new();
        var response = await httpClient.
GetFromJsonAsync<DABResponse<WarehouseItem>>("api/
WarehouseItems", cancellationToken:
cancellationToken);
        var pendingOrders = await httpClient.
GetFromJsonAsync<DABResponse<Order>>("api/
Orders?$filter=Status eq 'Pending'",
cancellationToken: cancellationToken);
        if (response != null && pendingOrders !=
null)
        {
            items.AddRange(response.Value.
Where(item => !pendingOrders.Value.Select(o =>
o.ItemID).Contains(item.ItemID)));
        }
        return items.ToArray();
    }
}

public record DABResponse<T>(List<T> Value);

public record WarehouseItem(int ItemID, string
ItemName, int Stock, DateTime LastUpdated);
```

```
public record Order(int OrderID, string
CustomerName, int ItemID, int Quantity, string
Status, DateTime OrderDate, DateTime LastUpdated);
```

The **DABResponse<T>** record models the typical structure of a paged response from DAB, containing a value property which is a list of the requested entities.

The **WarehouseClient** class was written by making use of a **primary constructor**, which allows you to define a constructor directly in the class declaration, making the code more concise. This means that when you create an instance of this class, you must pass an **HttpClient** object to it. The **HttpClient** is typically injected (dependency injection), which is a common practice in modern .NET applications to manage dependencies and improve testing.

This class contains a single method called **GetWarehouseStatus**. This method fetches the current status of warehouse items. It makes two asynchronous HTTP Get Requests using **HttpClient** to retrieve warehouse items and orders by invoking REST API endpoints created by DAB.

launchsettings.json

The **launchsettings.json** file is used to configure how the application is launched during development. This file is typically located in the properties folder of the project. It contains settings that define the environment variables, command line arguments, and profiles for running the application:

```
{
  "$schema": "http://json.schemastore.org/launchsettings.
json",
  "profiles": {
    "http": {
      "commandName": "Project",
      "dotnetRunMessages": true,
      "launchBrowser": true,
      "launchUrl": "api/warehousestatus",
      "applicationUrl": "http://localhost:5108",
      "environmentVariables": {
        "ASPNETCORE_ENVIRONMENT": "Development"
      }
```

```
    },
    "https": {
      "commandName": "Project",
      "dotnetRunMessages": true,
      "launchBrowser": true,
      "launchUrl": "api/warehousestatus",
      "applicationUrl": "https://localhost:7262;http://
localhost:5108",
      "environmentVariables": {
        "ASPNETCORE_ENVIRONMENT": "Development"
      }
    }
  }
}
```

Note: **The port numbers 7262 and 5108 are automatically generated, and you might see different port numbers when you create the API project.**

appsettings.json

The **appsettings.json** file is a configuration file used to store settings and configuration information in a structured format. This file is used to configure various aspects of the application, such as logging, connection strings, and custom settings:

```
{
  "Logging": {
    "LogLevel": {
      "Default": "Information",
      "Microsoft.AspNetCore": "Warning"
    }
  },
  "AllowedHosts": "*",
  "DabConfig": {
    "BaseUrlHttp": "http://localhost:5001/"
  }
}
```

Note: **The BaseUrlHttp refers to the port DAB listens on within its own container. .NET Aspire will manage exposing this service externally, often on a different port, and provides service discovery (e.g., https+http://dab) for other services to communicate with it.**

Program configuration

The **Program.cs** file is the entry point of the WarehouseAPI project, which sets up the necessary infrastructure for the Backend API, including dependency injection, middleware, routing, and configuration of services, and defines the HTTP request pipeline. It typically contains the main method, which is the starting point. However, from .NET 6 or later, the **Program.cs** file often uses top-level statements to simplify the code.

Since we created a WarehouseAPI project as a minimal API (without controllers), create a new GET endpoint **/api/warehousestatus** directly inside **Program.cs** and also configure the exception handler and map default endpoints. Full contents of the **Program.cs** files are shown in the following:

```
using System.Text.Json;
using WarehouseAPI;

var builder = WebApplication.CreateBuilder(args);

// Add service defaults & Aspire components.
builder.AddServiceDefaults();

// Add services to the container.
builder.Services.AddProblemDetails();

builder.Services.AddHttpClient<WarehouseClient>(client =>
    {
        // This URL uses "https+http://" to indicate
HTTPS is preferred over HTTP.
        // Learn more about service discovery scheme
resolution at https://aka.ms/dotnet/sdschemes.
        client.BaseAddress = new("https+http://dab");
    });

var app = builder.Build();

// Configure the HTTP request pipeline.
app.UseExceptionHandler();

app.MapGet("/api/warehousestatus", async (WarehouseClient
```

```
warehouseClient, HttpResponse response) =>
{
    var items = await warehouseClient.
GetWarehouseStatus();
    await JsonSerializer.SerializeAsync(response.Body,
items);
});
```

```
app.MapDefaultEndpoints();
```

```
app.Run();
```

WebApplication.CreateBuilder(args) initializes a new instance of the **WebApplicationBuilder** class, which sets up the application configuration, logging, and dependency injection.

Adding data API builder to the AppHost

Now that we have understood how DAB works, we need to add a SQL database and a DAB instance to our AppHost project.

Start by adding the needed references:

```
<Project Sdk="Microsoft.NET.Sdk">

  <Sdk Name="Aspire.AppHost.Sdk" Version="9.0.0-
rc.1.24511.1" />

  <PropertyGroup>
    <OutputType>Exe</OutputType>
    <TargetFramework>net8.0</TargetFramework>
    <ImplicitUsings>enable</ImplicitUsings>
    <Nullable>enable</Nullable>
    <IsAspireHost>true</IsAspireHost>
    <UserSecretsId>42534081-c920-4a7c-9716-a23d8cb0c4a1</
UserSecretsId>
  </PropertyGroup>

  <ItemGroup>
    <PackageReference Include="Aspire.Hosting.AppHost" />
```

```
    <PackageReference Include="Aspire.Hosting.SqlServer"
/>
    <PackageReference Include="CommunityToolkit.Aspire.
Hosting.Azure.DataApiBuilder" />
  </ItemGroup>

  <ItemGroup>
    <ProjectReference Include="..\..\WarehouseAPI\
WarehouseAPI.csproj" />
  </ItemGroup>

</Project>
```

In the **Eshop.AppHost/Program.cs**, we can add the following code:

```
var builder = DistributedApplication.CreateBuilder(args);

// Add a SQL Server container
var sqlPassword = builder.AddParameter("sql-password");
var sqlServer = builder
    .AddSqlServer("sql", sqlPassword);

// uncomment this line to persist the database between
runs
sqlServer.WithLifetime(ContainerLifetime.Persistent);

var sqlDatabase = sqlServer.AddDatabase("WarehouseDB");

// Populate the database with the schema and data
sqlServer
    .WithBindMount("./sql-server", target: "/usr/config")
    .WithBindMount("../../../db-scripts", target: "/
docker-entrypoint-initdb.d")
    .WithEntrypoint("/usr/config/entrypoint.sh");

var dab = builder.AddDataAPIBuilder("dab", "../../../dab/
dab-config.json")
    .WithReference(sqlDatabase)
    .WaitFor(sqlServer);

builder.AddProject<Projects.WarehouseAPI>("warehouseapi")
    .WithReference(dab)
```

```
    .WaitFor(dab);

builder.Build().Run();
```

There are several new things introduced in this piece of code. In line **.AddSqlServer("sql", sqlPassword);**, we add a parameter that will hold the SQL database password. This parameter is defined in the **appsettings.json** file of the AppHost project:

```
{
  "Logging": {
    "LogLevel": {
      "Default": "Information",
      "Microsoft.AspNetCore": "Warning",
      "Aspire.Hosting.Dcp": "Warning"
    }
  },
  "Parameters": {
    "sql-password": "P_ssw0rd!"
  }
}
```

Then, we can find the lines to add a SQL Server, which we called **SQL**. This is a hosting resource that will create a new instance of a local SQL Server container.

The following line handles the lifetime of the SQL container. Since every time the application starts we will seed the database, we can leverage the .NET Aspire container lifetime management to persist the container between different executions.

sqlServer.WithLifetime(ContainerLifetime.Persistent);

Once we have a persistent SQL Server, we can add a database to that server, which we call **WarehouseDB**.

Now all we need to do is seed the database, and we will use some scripts provided by Jerry Nixon in a public GitHub repository: **https://github.com/JerryNixon/aspire-sqlserver/tree/main/202411-DotnetConf**.

To use these scripts, create a **sql-server** folder inside the **Eshop.AppHost** folder and create **configure-db.sh** and **entrypoint.sh**.

- **configure-db.sh**: This script waits for SQL Server to be ready and then executes any **.sql** files found in **/docker-entrypoint-initdb.d** to set up databases and schemas.

- **entrypoint.sh**: This is the main entry point for the SQL Server container. It starts the **configure-db.sh** script in the background and then launches the SQL Server process itself.

Make sure both files use the **LF** (**Line Feed**) termination character and are marked as executable in Linux.

In the **configure-db.sh** paste the below code:

```
#!/bin/bash

# set -x

# Adapted from: https://github.com/microsoft/mssql-
docker/blob/80e2a51d0eb1693f2de014fb26d4a414f5a5add5/
linux/preview/examples/mssql-customize/configure-db.sh

# Wait 60 seconds for SQL Server to start up by ensuring
that
# calling SQLCMD does not return an error code, which
will ensure that sqlcmd is accessible
# and that system and user databases return "0" which
means all databases are in an "online" state
# https://docs.microsoft.com/en-us/sql/relational-
databases/system-catalog-views/sys-databases-transact-
sql?view=sql-server-2017

dbstatus=1
errcode=1
start_time=$SECONDS
end_by=$((start_time + 60))

echo "Starting check for SQL Server start-up at $start_
time, will end at $end_by"

while [[ $SECONDS -lt $end_by && ( $errcode -ne 0 || ( -z
"$dbstatus" || $dbstatus -ne 0 ) ) ]]; do
    dbstatus="$(/opt/mssql-tools18/bin/sqlcmd -h -1 -t
1 -U sa -P "$MSSQL_SA_PASSWORD" -C -Q "SET NOCOUNT ON;
```

```
Select SUM(state) from sys.databases")"
    errcode=$?
    sleep 1
done

elapsed_time=$((SECONDS - start_time))
echo "Stopped checking for SQL Server
start-up after $elapsed_time seconds
(dbstatus=$dbstatus,errcode=$errcode,seconds=$SECONDS)"

if [[ $dbstatus -ne 0 ]] || [[ $errcode -ne 0 ]]; then
    echo "SQL Server took more than 60 seconds to start
up or one or more databases are not in an ONLINE state"
    echo "dbstatus = $dbstatus"
    echo "errcode = $errcode"
    exit 1
fi

# Loop through the .sql files in the root of /docker-
entrypoint-initdb.d and execute them with sqlcmd
for f in $(find /docker-entrypoint-initdb.d -maxdepth 1
-type f -name "*.sql" | sort); do
    echo "- A -=- Processing $f file..."
    /opt/mssql-tools18/bin/sqlcmd -S localhost -U sa -P
"$MSSQL_SA_PASSWORD" -C -d master -i "$f"
done

# Loop through each subdirectory in /docker-entrypoint-
initdb.d
for dir in $(find /docker-entrypoint-initdb.d -mindepth 1
-maxdepth 1 -type d | sort); do
    # Loop through the .sql files in each subdirectory and
execute them with sqlcmd
    for f in $(find "$dir" -maxdepth 1 -type f -name
"*.sql" | sort); do
        echo "- B -=- Processing $f file in directory
$dir..."
        /opt/mssql-tools18/bin/sqlcmd -S localhost -U sa
-P "$MSSQL_SA_PASSWORD" -C -d master -i "$f"
    done
done
```

In the **entrypoint.sh** paste the following code:

```bash
#!/bin/bash

# Start the script to create the DB and user
/usr/config/configure-db.sh &

# Start SQL Server
/opt/mssql/bin/sqlservr
```

In the root folder of your solution, create a **db-scripts** folder and add a **warehousedb.sql** file, as shown in the following:

```sql
-- SQL script to create the Warehouse database and table
USE [master]
GO

CREATE DATABASE [WarehouseDB]
GO

USE [WarehouseDB]
GO

-- create warehouseitems table
CREATE TABLE WarehouseItems (
    ItemID INT PRIMARY KEY IDENTITY(1,1),
    ItemName NVARCHAR(100) NOT NULL,
    Stock INT NOT NULL,
    LastUpdated DATETIME DEFAULT GETDATE()
);

-- create orders table
CREATE TABLE Orders (
    OrderID INT PRIMARY KEY IDENTITY(1,1),
    CustomerName NVARCHAR(100) NOT NULL,
    ItemID INT NOT NULL,
    Quantity INT NOT NULL,
    Status NVARCHAR(50) CHECK (Status IN ('Pending',
'Processing', 'Completed')),
    OrderDate DATETIME DEFAULT GETDATE(),
    LastUpdated DATETIME DEFAULT GETDATE()
```

```
);

-- Foreign key to link to Warehouse items
ALTER TABLE Orders
ADD FOREIGN KEY (ItemID) REFERENCES WarehouseDB.dbo.
WarehouseItems(ItemID);

-- Insert a row into orders table by creating a sample
processing order for the Tablet
INSERT INTO dbo.Orders (CustomerName, ItemID,
LastUpdated, OrderDate, Quantity, Status)
SELECT 'John Doe', ItemID, GETDATE(), GETDATE(), 10,
'Processing'
FROM dbo.WarehouseItems
WHERE ItemName = 'Tablet'
;

-- Insert sample data into warehouseitems
INSERT INTO WarehouseItems (ItemName, Stock) VALUES
('Laptop', 50),
('Smartphone', 100),
('Tablet', 75);
```

All these scripts are needed to populate the database when we run
the project, and are used in the **Eshop.AppHost/Program.cs**:

```
sqlServer
    .WithBindMount("./sql-server", target: "/usr/config")
    .WithBindMount("../../../db-scripts", target: "/
docker-entrypoint-initdb.d")
    .WithEntrypoint("/usr/config/entrypoint.sh");
```

Now we have a locally containerized database that we can expose
using DAB. DAB has been added to our AppHost as a hosting
Integration like this:

```
var dab = builder.AddDataAPIBuilder("dab", "../../../dab/
dab-config.json")
    .WithReference(sqlDatabase)
    .WaitFor(sqlServer);
```

Note that the DAB resource is referencing the database resource and is waiting for the SQL server resource. This is because DAB needs to wait for the SQL server to be available before it starts, and it needs to reference the connection string to the database. This will cause .NET Aspire to inject inside the container the environment variable **ConnectionStrings__WarehouseDB**, the same variable we have referenced in the **dab-config.json**.

The **AddDataAPIBuilder** method comes from the package named **CommunityToolkit.Aspire.Hosting.Azure.DataApiBuilder**. You may notice that this is an Aspire hosting integration, but the package name starts with **CommunityToolkit**. This is because this integration is not provided by the official .NET Aspire team.

.NET Aspire Community Toolkit

The .NET Aspire product group focuses its attention on the development of Aspire itself and a few core integrations. However, they alone cannot keep up with all the different resources that might be needed in a distributed application solution. That is why the community started to work on the .NET Aspire Community Toolkit. It is a public repository in which the community is interested in extending .NET Aspire works to share different custom integrations, such as the one we are using for DAB. Under the hood, that integration simply uses the standard Container resource type provided by .NET Aspire to define a preconfigured container of DAB. This is not that different from what **Aspire.Hosting.Redis** integration we have seen before.

Running Eshop Aspire from Visual Studio

If you have followed until here, you would also have the same code on your local development machine. Right-click on the **Eshop. AppHost** project and select **Set as Start up Project**. Make sure the Docker engine is running by checking the docker desktop app. Press *F5* or the green start button on the top pane of Visual Studio to run your Eshop Application. A console window is opened, as shown in *Figure 2.9*, which contains detailed logs about the application and also a link to the Aspire dashboard:

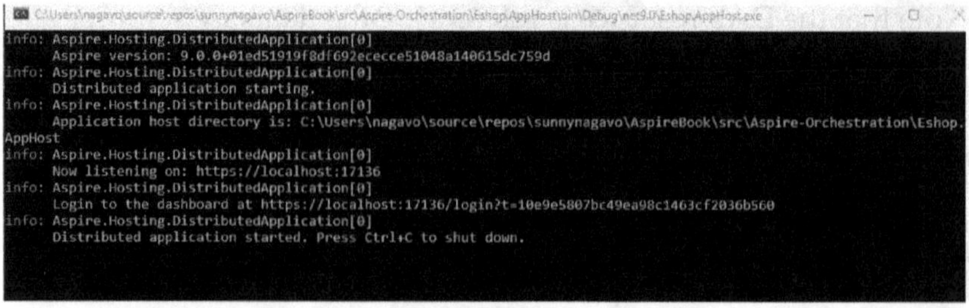

Figure 2.9: Console window displaying Aspire app host logs

A browser window is also opened with an endpoint displayed in the console window **https://localhost:17136**, which displays the resources view as shown in *Figure 2.10*:

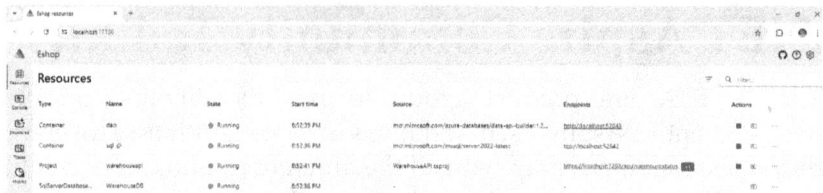

Figure 2.10: .NET Aspire dashboard displaying resources view

If you monitor during the .NET Aspire page load, SQL containers will have started running first, followed by DAB, followed by the WarehouseAPI project since we use the **.WaitFor()** method in code. **WaitFor** (dependency object) method waits for the dependency resource to enter the running state before starting the resource. This is useful when a resource should wait until another has started running. This can help reduce errors in logs during local development due to dependencies. Let us use .http files within Visual Studio to test the WarehouseAPI by invoking their endpoints.

Use .http files in Visual Studio to validate API

The Visual Studio team has added **.http** file editor support, which is a convenient way to test ASP.NET API projects by sending HTTP requests directly within the IDE without needing external tools like postman, insomnia, or curl. A file can contain multiple requests by using lines with ### as delimiters. The following example shows a GET request to the **https://localhost:7262/api/ warehousestatus** endpoint:

```
@WarehouseAPI_HostAddress = https://localhost:7262

GET {{WarehouseAPI_HostAddress}}/api/warehousestatus
Accept: application/json
```

By clicking **Send**, the request will make a HTTP request, and the response is returned as JSON within a side pane as shown in *Figure 2.11*:

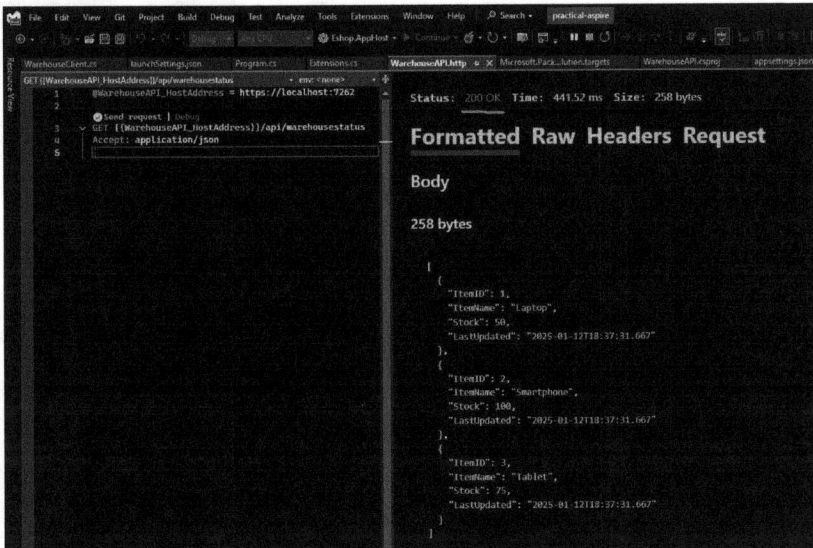

Figure 2.11: Receiving JSON response by sending a request from .http file

Conclusion

In this chapter, we explored the .NET Aspire integrations and their benefits. We explained step-by-step instructions along with code files on how to create a .NET Aspire empty solution using the predefined .NET Aspire project template and add our first Web API project in .NET (**WarehouseAPI**). We briefly discussed DAB and how to install and use them in our API code to take advantage of talking to databases without writing a bunch of code.

In the next chapter, we will discuss how to leverage multi-language support (for example, Python, Golang, Node.js) to write different services and how .NET Aspire helps in integrating and bringing them under one umbrella which makes it easy to monitor and help in running and debugging these microservices within your local development environment.

Join our Discord space

Join our Discord workspace for latest updates, offers, tech happenings around the world, new releases, and sessions with the authors:

https://discord.bpbonline.com

CHAPTER 3
.NET Aspire and Other Languages

Introduction

In *Chapter 2, .NET Aspire Integrations*, we utilized the .NET framework to build our first backend service. However, the power of microservice architecture lies in the magic of leveraging the best tools and frameworks for building each specific component without depending on only one ecosystem. Integrating multiple programming languages can be beneficial for optimizing performance, scalability, and maintainability. This chapter explores how .NET Aspire seamlessly integrates with services written in other languages, such as Python, Go, and Node.js, enabling it to build a polyglot microservice.

Structure

In this chapter, we will discuss the following topics:

- Setting up a development environment
- Benefits of a polyglot microservices architecture

- Integrating service with .NET Aspire
- Implementing different microservices
- Orchestrating external services with .NET Aspire

Objectives

By the end of the chapter, you will learn about how to leverage other programming languages such as Python, Go, and Node.js to build polyglot microservices. You will also leverage .NET Aspire for local debugging as well as to deploy these services in production.

Let us look into some prerequisites before we begin.

Setting up a development environment

Since we are considering utilizing multiple languages, make sure you have your development environment set up and configured by installing or setting up the following resources.

- An Azure account with an active subscription **https:// azure.microsoft.com/free/?ref=microsoft.com&utm_ source=microsoft.com&utm_medium=docs&utm_ campaign=visualstudio**

- .NET Aspire SDK **https://learn.microsoft.com/en-us/dotnet/ aspire/fundamentals/dotnet-aspire-sdk**

- PowerShell 7.0 or higher version (For Windows users only) **https://learn.microsoft.com/en-us/ powershell/scripting/install/installing-powershell-on-windows?view=powershell-7.4#installing-the-msi-package**

- Go SDK **https://go.dev/dl/**

- Install Python **https://www.python.org/downloads/**

- Node.js SDK **https://nodejs.org/en/download**

- Docker Desktop **https://docs.docker.com/desktop/install/ windows-install/**

- Visual Studio Code **https://code.visualstudio.com/ (or) Visual Studio 2022 https://visualstudio.microsoft.com/vs/**

- VS Code Docker extension **https://marketplace.visualstudio. com/items?itemName=ms-azuretools.vscode-docker**

Benefits of a polyglot microservices architecture

A polyglot approach to microservices, where different microservices are written in different programming languages, provides advantages over writing in a single language setting:

- **Flexibility and optimal tool selection**: Each programming language has its own strengths and weaknesses. A polyglot architecture lets you pick the perfect language for each microservice based on its specific needs, ensuring you're using the best tool for the job.

- **Enhanced performance**: Certain languages are simply more fitted to certain tasks. For example, Go excels at concurrency and speed, making it a great choice for high-performance microservices, while Python's simplicity can be ideal for data processing tasks.

- **Scalability**: Different languages handle scaling differently. Node.js, for instance, is known for its ability to manage a high volume of requests, making it a popular choice for microservices that need to scale quickly.

- **Maintainability**: Microservices written in different languages are inherently more modular. This allows each microservice to be developed, tested, and deployed independently, making the overall system easier to maintain and update compared to a monolithic application in a single language.

- **Attracting diverse talent**: Finding developers with expertise in a specific language is often easier than finding those proficient in multiple languages. A polyglot architecture broadens your talent pool, allowing you to attract developers with diverse skill sets.

Integrating services with .NET Aspire

As mentioned in the previous chapters, .NET Aspire supports resources of three different types:

- **.NET projects** are the standard way to integrate .NET applications into a .NET Aspire Solution. They provide a seamless developer experience along with built-in debugging and service discovery.

- **Containers** allow you to run applications packaged in Docker containers with .NET Aspire.

- **Executables** enable .NET Aspire to support and orchestrate projects written in different programming languages alongside .NET projects.

Both Executable and Container resources enable .NET Aspire to support projects of different programming languages. Considering the Container resource first, we could write a Dockerfile for our Node. js project and run it with .NET Aspire as a container. However, that would not allow for a seamless developer experience. Every change would require a full container rebuild before being able to run our solution. By running applications as executables, .NET Aspire can manage and orchestrate them alongside .NET projects. That is why we will focus on integrating other languages using the executable resources in this chapter.

Implementing different microservices

As mentioned in the reference architecture in *Chapter 1, Introduction to .NET Aspire*, we will discuss the implementation details of three microservices:

- **Create order API**: Implemented in Golang, this service handles the creation of new orders. When a request is made to the create order API, it will create a new order in the order database and set it to pending.

- **Payment API**: Implemented in Python, this service processes payments for orders. When a request is made to the payment API, it will set the order status to processing.

- **Shipping API**: Implemented in Node.js, this service manages the shipping of orders. When a request is made to the shipping API, it will set the order status to completion.

Before beginning with project creation, make sure all the prerequisites are installed on your machine.

The following are the steps to creating an order API in Go:

1. Open cmd prompt and create the project directory **create-order-api** inside the SRC folder:

```
mkdir create-order-api
Cd create-order-api
```

2. Initialize Go module:

```
go mod init create-order-api
```

3. Create a **main.go** file to implement the **create-order-api** endpoint, as shown in the following. To avoid excessive code, we are showing only the key method. The full code is available on our GitHub repository.

```
var db = make(map[string]string)


//OpenTelemetry metrics meter and
metricRequestTotal is initialized later in the full
application
var (
        name                    = os.Getenv("OTEL_
SERVICE_NAME")
        isInsecure              bool
        otelTarget              string
        headers                 map[string]string
        meter                   metric.Meter
        metricRequestTotal      metric.Int64Counter
        responseTimeHistogram metric.Int64Histogram
)


func setupRouter() *gin.Engine {
```

```
// Disable Console Color
// gin.DisableConsoleColor()

r := gin.Default()
r.Use(otelgin.Middleware(name))
r.Use(monitorInterceptor())

// Ping test
r.GET("/ping", func(c *gin.Context) {
        c.String(http.StatusOK, "pong")
})

r.POST("api/create-order", func(c *gin.
Context) {
        // Parse JSON
        var order struct {
CustomerName string `json:"CustomerName"
binding:"required"`
ItemID string `json:"ItemID" binding:"required"`
Quantity int `json:"Quantity" binding:"required"`
Status string `json:"Status" binding:"required"`
OrderDate string `json:"OrderDate" binding:"required"`
LastUpdated string `json:"LastUpdated"
binding:"required"`
        }

        if err := c.ShouldBindJSON(&order);
err != nil {
                c.JSON(http.StatusBadRequest,
gin.H{"error": err.Error()})
                return
        }

        order.OrderDate = time.Now().
Format(time.RFC3339)
        order.LastUpdated = time.Now().
Format(time.RFC3339)

        client := &http.Client{}
        reqBody, err := json.Marshal(order)
        if err != nil {
```

```go
                        c.JSON(http.
StatusInternalServerError, gin.H{"error": "Failed
to marshal order data"})
                        return
                }


                req, err := http.NewRequest("POST",
os.Getenv("services__dab__http__0")+"/api/Orders",
strings.NewReader(string(reqBody)))
                if err != nil {
                        c.JSON(http.
StatusInternalServerError, gin.H{"error": "Failed
to create request"})
                        return
                }
                req.Header.Set("Content-Type",
"application/json")

                resp, err := client.Do(req)
                if err != nil {
                        c.JSON(http.
StatusInternalServerError, gin.H{"error": "Failed
to send request"})
                        return
                }
                defer resp.Body.Close()

                if resp.StatusCode != http.
StatusCreated {
                        c.JSON(resp.StatusCode,
gin.H{"error": "Failed to create order"})
                        return
                }

                c.JSON(http.StatusCreated,
gin.H{"status": "order created"})
        })

        return r
}
```

The above code sets up a Gin web server with an endpoint that receives order data. It then sends that data to the DAB endpoint, whose address is retrieved from an environment variable **services__dab__http__0,** likely provided by .NET Aspire. We return a success or error response based on the result from the DAB service.

4. To run the application:

```
go run main.go
```

The following are the steps in processing payments with Python:

1. Open the cmd prompt and create the project directory **process-payment-api** inside the SRC folder.

```
mkdir process-payment-api
cd process-payment-api
```

2. Create a virtual environment and activate it (optional but recommended):

```
python3 -m venv venv
source venv/bin/activate
```

3. Install dependencies:

```
pip install fastapi uvicorn
```

4. Create a new file named **__init__.py** under the **process-payment-api** folder with the contents as shown in the following.

```
from fastapi import FastAPI, HTTPException
from pydantic import BaseModel
import uvicorn
import os
import requests
from datetime import datetime

app = FastAPI()

class PaymentPayload(BaseModel):
    OrderID: str

@app.post("/api/process-payment")
```

```python
def process_payment(payload: PaymentPayload):
    order_id = payload.OrderID
    if not order_id:
        raise HTTPException(status_code=400,
detail="Payload must contain 'OrderID'")

    api_endpoint = os.environ.get("services__dab__
http__0")
    if not api_endpoint:
        raise HTTPException(status_code=500,
detail="Environment variable 'services__dab__
http__0' is not set")

    # Read the order with OrderID from the same
endpoint
    url = f"{api_endpoint}/api/Orders/OrderID/
{order_id}"
    response = requests.get(url)
    if response.status_code != 200:
        raise HTTPException(status_code=500,
detail=f"Failed to retrieve order: {response.
text}")

    order_data = response.json()

    # Extract the first item from the array
    order_data = order_data["value"][0]

    # Remove the OrderID field from the order data
    if "OrderID" in order_data:
        del order_data["OrderID"]
    # Update the order data
    order_data["Status"] = "processing"
    order_data["LastUpdated"] = datetime.utcnow().
isoformat()

    # Print the updated order data for debug
purposes
    print("Updated order data:", order_data)

    # Send the updated order data as an update
```

```
request
    response = requests.put(url, json=order_data)
    if response.status_code != 200:
        raise HTTPException(status_code=500,
detail=f"Failed to update order status: {response.
text}")

    return response.json()

def main() -> None:
    port = int(os.environ.get("PORT", 8000))
    uvicorn.run(app, host="127.0.0.1", port=port)
```

The above code handles POST requests to **/api/process-payment** by handling the incoming payload. It retrieves the order details from the DAB service using the order ID, updates the order status to **Processing,** and sends the updated order data back to the caller. HTTP errors are raised if any step fails.

Inside the **Main** function, it runs the FAST API application using uvicorn on the specified port.

5. To run the Process-Payment Python service independently (outside Docker/Orchestration), navigate to the **src/process-payment-api/src** directory and execute the following command:

```
python -m process_payment_api
```

This command works because the **__init__.py** file defines a **main()** function. Make sure all the required dependencies (FASTAPI, uvicorn, pydantic etc.) are installed and set the necessary environment variable **sercices__dab__http__0** (endpoint for the DAB).

Note: **Architecture diagram to understand the interaction between different polyglot microservices, please refer to Figure 1.12 in Chapter 1, Introduction to .NET Aspire.**

The steps for creating a shipping API with Node.js are as follows:

1. Open the cmd prompt and create the project directory **shipping-api** inside the SRC folder.

```
mkdir shipping-api
cd shipping-api
```

2. Initialize a Node.js project:

```
npm init -y
```

3. Install Express and other required packages:

```
npm install express axios body-parser
```

4. Create a new file called **index.js** with the contents as shown in the following:

```
const express = require('express');
const axios = require('axios');
const bodyParser = require('body-parser');

const app = express();
app.use(bodyParser.json());

app.post('/api/ship-product', async (req, res) => {
    const { OrderID } = req.body;
    if (!OrderID) {
        return res.status(400).json({ detail:
"Payload must contain 'OrderID'" });
    }

    const apiEndpoint = process.env.services__dab__
http__0;
    if (!apiEndpoint) {
        return res.status(500).json({ detail:
"Environment variable 'services__dab__http__0' is
not set" });
    }

    try {
        // Read the order with OrderID from the
same endpoint
        const url = `${apiEndpoint}/api/Orders/
OrderID/${OrderID}`;
        let response = await axios.get(url);
        if (response.status !== 200) {
            return res.status(500).json({ detail:
```

```
        `Failed to retrieve order: ${response.data}` });
        }

        let orderData = response.data.value[0];

        // Remove the OrderID field from the order
data
        delete orderData.OrderID;

        // Update the order data
        orderData.Status = "completed";
        orderData.LastUpdated = new Date().
toISOString();

        // Print the updated order data for debug
purposes
        console.log("Updated order data:", JSON.
stringify(orderData, null, 2));

        // Update the order data
        const config = {
            headers: {
                'Content-Type': 'application/json'
            }
        };
        response = await axios.put(url, JSON.
stringify(orderData, null, 2), config);

        // Update the warehouse stock based on the
order details
        const warehouseUrl = `${apiEndpoint}/api/
WarehouseItems/ItemID/${orderData.ItemID}`;
        let warehouseResponse = await axios.
get(warehouseUrl);
        let warehouseItem = warehouseResponse.data.
value[0];
        warehouseItem.Stock -= orderData.Quantity;
        delete warehouseItem.ItemID;

        // Print the updated warehouese quantity
for debug purposes
```

```
        console.log("Updated warehouse data:",
JSON.stringify(warehouseItem, null, 2));

        await axios.put(warehouseUrl, JSON.
stringify(warehouseItem, null, 2), config);

        res.json(response.data);
    } catch (error) {
        res.status(500).json({ detail: `Error
processing request: ${error.message}` });
    }
});

const port = process.env.PORT || 8000;
app.listen(port, () => {
    console.log(`Server is running on port
${port}`);
});
```

The above code uses the Express library to create the web server and axios to make HTTP requests to the DAB service. The API listens for POST requests on the **/api/ship-product** endpoint. When a request is received, it first checks for **OrderId**. If not, it returns an error response. The code then retrieves the DAB endpoint from the **Services_dab_http_0** environment variable. It then makes a GET request to DAB to retrieve the order details for the given **OrderId**. If the order is found, the order status is updated to **Completed**, along with the **LastUpdated** timestamp. It then makes a PUT request to the DAB service to update the order in the database and also decrement the warehouse item stock by the order quantity. The code returns a successful response if all of the steps are successful; otherwise, it returns an error response if any of the steps fail.

5. To run the application:

node index.js

Orchestrating external services with .NET Aspire

While these microservices can be run independently, our primary goal is to integrate them into our existing .NET Aspire project for its advantages. Firstly, we will take a look at the signature method to add an executable resource, which is simple enough on its own:

```
public static IResourceBuilder<ExecutableResource>
AddExecutable(this IDistributedApplicationBuilder
builder, [ResourceName] string name, string command,
string workingDirectory, params object[]? args)
```

As per every other resource, the first required parameter is the name of the resource. We also need a command (that would be **go** for Golang, **node** for Node.js, and so on) and a working directory, which is the path in which we want to launch that command. The last parameter is an optional list of parameters we might want to pass to our command. If we consider a Golang project, to actually run it, we cannot simply run the **go** command in the project directory. We need to launch the command **go run**, which means **run everything in this folder**.

Using the **AddExecutable** method, adding a generic Golang program to our **AppHost** project would result in something like:

```
builder.AddExecutable("my-golang-app", "go", "path/to/
golang/app", "run", ".");
```

We have not yet discussed the way .NET Aspire can be used to deploy our distributed application to the cloud, but in the meantime, we are missing something that would break this functionality. We are not describing how that resource should be published. An executable on its own is not a recognized resource that can be deployed to the cloud. That is why we need to add **PublishAsDockerfile()**:

```
builder.AddExecutable("my-golang-app", "go", "path/to/
golang/app", "run", ".")
    .PublishAsDockerFile();
```

This way, we are telling our **DistributedApplication** builder that this executable resource should be published as a container during deployment. If not otherwise specified, the Dockerfile is expected to be found in the working directory.

If we want to be able to monitor our resource via OpenTelemetry, we might also add **WithOtlpExporter**:

```
builder.AddExecutable("my-golang-app", "go", "path/to/
golang/app", "run", ".")
    .WithOtlpExporter()
    .PublishAsDockerFile();
```

This will inject the necessary environment variables to connect our program to the open telemetry endpoints provided by .NET Aspire.

Also, since we are working on a distributed application, our executable resource will probably require some endpoint. We, therefore, need to instruct .NET Aspire on how to map the ports of this resource. To achieve this, we use the **WithHttpEndpoint** or **WithHttpsEndpoint** for local HTTPS:

```
public static IResourceBuilder<T>
WithHttpEndpoint<T>(this IResourceBuilder<T> builder,
int? port = null, int? targetPort = null, string? name =
null, string? env = null, bool isProxied = true) where T
: IResourceWithEndpoints
```

Going through each parameter:

- **port**: An optional port. This is the port that will be given to the other resources to communicate with this resource.

- **targetPort**: This is the port the resource is listening on.

- **name**: An optional name of the endpoint. Defaults to **http** or **https** when using **WithHttpsEndpoint** if not specified.

- **env**: An optional name of the environment variable to inject.

- **isProxied**: Specifies if the endpoint will be proxied by DCP. Defaults to true.

Suppose our **golang** application was a web server listening on port 5000, we could then add this line:

```
var golang = builder.AddExecutable("my-golang-app", "go",
"path/to/golang/app", "run", ".")
    .WithHttpEndpoint(port: 5001, targetPort: 5000)
    .WithOtlpExporter()
    .PublishAsDockerFile();
```

If we wanted to let .NET Aspire choose a random port for our program and also use a random port to start our web server, we can write as follows:

```
var golang = builder.AddExecutable("my-golang-app", "go",
"path/to/golang/app", "run", ".")
    .WithHttpEndpoint(env: "PORT")
    .WithOtlpExporter()
    .PublishAsDockerFile();
```

In this scenario, .NET Aspire will still generate two random ports, one of which will be injected into our resource so that we can use it when we start the web server. The other will be the port used by other resources to call our Golang program. This approach is usually the preferred one since we cannot always be sure about which port is available on our machine (or another developer's machine with whom we might want to share our project).

The last bit we are missing to have a fully working integration is to share our Golang resource endpoint with other resources. Since the executable resource is not a resource that necessarily implies an **http** endpoint, we cannot simply use **WithReference(golang)** as we would normally do. We need to retrieve the resource http endpoint and pass that as a reference where needed:

```
var golang = builder.AddExecutable("my-golang-app", "go",
"path/to/golang/app", "run", ".")
    .WithHttpEndpoint(name: "PORT")
    .WithOtlpExporter()
    .PublishAsDockerFile();
var golangEndpoint = golang.GetEndpoint("http");

builder.AddProject<Projects.Test_Web>("webfrontend")
    .WithReference(golangEndpoint);
```

These are a lot of steps for adding a simple executable to our distributed application, especially if we compare this to the single line of code we need to write when dealing with a .NET project:

```
var apiService = builder.AddProject<Projects.Test_
ApiService>("apiservice");
```

The beauty of .NET, though, is that we can wrap everything in a method and ship it as a NuGet package. You could expect to find something easier to use, for instance:

```
var golangApp = builder.AddGolangApp("my-golang-app",
"path/to/golang/app")
    .WithHttpEndpoint(env: "PORT");
```

To use a method as **AddGolangApp** we need to rely on the .NET Aspire Community Toolkit. The application we are trying to build requires Golang, Node.js, Python (using the **uv** package manager), and React. React and Node.js are provided by standard .NET Aspire integrations, available by adding the below NuGet package **Aspire. Hosting.NodeJS** to our AppHost project:

```
<PackageReference Include="Aspire.Hosting.NodeJS" />
```

From the Community Toolkit, we can add these packages:

```
<PackageReference Include="CommunityToolkit.Aspire.
Hosting.Golang" />
<PackageReference Include="CommunityToolkit.Aspire.Hosting.
Python.Extensions"/>
<PackageReference Include="CommunityToolkit.Aspire.Hosting.
NodeJS.Extensions"/>
```

You might notice that both Python and Node.js package names end with **.Extensions**. That is because Python and Node.js are natively supported by .NET Aspire packages. However, we are not using standard Python apps in our architecture, but rather **Uv**, as previously mentioned. To run **Uv** modules, we need to use **CommunityToolkit.Aspire.Hosting.Python.Extensions**. Also, the **CommunityToolkit.Aspire.Hosting.NodeJS.Extensions** provide some useful extension methods to automatically install node modules when we run the AppHost project.

Now that we have everything we need from .NET Aspire and the **CommunityToolkit**, we can add the remaining resources to our **Eshop.AppHost** project in the **Program.cs**:

```
var createOrderApi = builder.AddGolangApp("create-order",
"../../create-order-api")
    .WithHttpEndpoint(port: 5001, env: "PORT")
    .WithReference(dab)
    .WaitFor(dab);

var processPaymentApi = builder.AddUvApp("process-
payment", "../../process-payment-api", "process-payment-
```

```
api")
    .WithHttpEndpoint(port: 5002, env: "PORT")
    .WithReference(dab)
    .WaitFor(dab);

var shippingApi = builder.AddNodeApp("ship-api", "index.
js", "../../shipping-api/src")
    .WithNpmPackageInstallation()
    .WithHttpEndpoint(port: 5003, env: "PORT")
    .WithReference(dab)
    .WaitFor(dab);

// Add the React front-end project
builder.AddNpmApp("FrontendWithReact", "../../
FrontendWithReact/frontend-react-app")
    .WithNpmPackageInstallation()
    .WithReference(warehouseApi)
    .WaitFor(warehouseApi)
    .WithReference(createOrderApi)
    .WaitFor(createOrderApi)
    .WithReference(processPaymentApi)
    .WaitFor(processPaymentApi)
    .WithReference(shippingApi)
    .WaitFor(shippingApi)
    .WithHttpEndpoint(env: "PORT")
    .WithEnvironment("BROWSER", "none") // Disable
opening browser on npm start
    .WithExternalHttpEndpoints()
    .WaitFor(dab)
    .PublishAsDockerFile();
```

We can take a look under the hood and see what a method such as **AddGolangApp** actually does. Of course, it is not just a simple wrapper for the **AddExecutable** we have seen before, but the logic is the same:

```
public static
IResourceBuilder<GolangAppExecutableResource>
AddGolangApp(this IDistributedApplicationBuilder builder,
[ResourceName] string name, string workingDirectory,
string[]? args = null)
    {
```

```
      ArgumentNullException.ThrowIfNull(builder,
nameof(builder));
      ArgumentException.ThrowIfNullOrWhiteSpace(name,
nameof(name));
      ArgumentException.
ThrowIfNullOrWhiteSpace(workingDirectory,
nameof(workingDirectory));

      string[] allArgs = args is { Length: > 0 }
          ? ["run", ".", .. args]
          : ["run", ".",];

      workingDirectory = Path.Combine(builder.
AppHostDirectory, workingDirectory).
NormalizePathForCurrentPlatform();
      var resource = new
GolangAppExecutableResource(name, workingDirectory);

      return builder.AddResource(resource)
                .WithGolangDefaults()
                .WithArgs(allArgs);
   }
```

It starts by defining an array of arguments. Those arguments have the hardcoded values of **"run"** and **"."** and optional arguments that the developer might want to pass to the command are appended. Then, it creates a **GolangAppExecutableResource**:

```
public class GolangAppExecutableResource(string name,
string workingDirectory)
    : ExecutableResource(name, "go", workingDirectory),
IResourceWithServiceDiscovery;
```

This class extends the **ExecutableResource**, hardcoding the **go** command, and inherits from **IResourceWithServiceDiscovery**. This will allow the **GolangAppExecutableResource** object to be referenced directly by other resources without the need to extract its endpoint every time.

To this resource, we add some default configuration using the **WithGolangDefaults**, which is an extension method that, in this case, adds the **OtlpExporter**:

```
private static
IResourceBuilder<GolangAppExecutableResource>
WithGolangDefaults(
        this IResourceBuilder<GolangAppExecutableResource>
builder) =>
        builder.WithOtlpExporter();
```

Lastly, we append the arguments using the **WithArgs(allArgs)** method. This will result in an executable resource that can expose endpoints to other resources with open telemetry environment variables and that will run the command **go run** in a given folder.

All the other methods work in the same way, taking into account the different nuances of each language. For instance, Python has a slightly more complicated command build pipeline because we need to consider the Python version specified in the virtual environment and the different parameters we need to use when running the application with open telemetry.

Therefore, the **AddUvApp** looks like this:

```
public static IResourceBuilder<UvAppResource> AddUvApp(
        this IDistributedApplicationBuilder builder,
        string name,
        string projectDirectory,
        string scriptPath,
        params string[] scriptArgs)
    {

        ArgumentNullException.ThrowIfNull(builder);

        return builder.AddUvApp(name, scriptPath,
projectDirectory, ".venv", scriptArgs);
    }

    private static IResourceBuilder<UvAppResource>
AddUvApp(this IDistributedApplicationBuilder builder,
        string name,
        string scriptPath,
        string projectDirectory,
        string virtualEnvironmentPath,
        params string[] args)
    {

        ArgumentNullException.ThrowIfNull(builder);
```

```
ArgumentNullException.ThrowIfNull(name);
ArgumentNullException.ThrowIfNull(scriptPath);

        string wd = projectDirectory ?? Path.
Combine("..", name);

        projectDirectory = PathNormalizer.
NormalizePathForCurrentPlatform(Path.Combine(builder.
AppHostDirectory, wd));

        var virtualEnvironment
= new VirtualEnvironment(Path.
IsPathRooted(virtualEnvironmentPath)
            ? virtualEnvironmentPath
            : Path.Join(projectDirectory,
virtualEnvironmentPath));

        var instrumentationExecutable =
virtualEnvironment.GetExecutable("opentelemetry-
instrument");
        // var pythonExecutable = virtualEnvironment.
GetRequiredExecutable("python");
        // var projectExecutable =
instrumentationExecutable ?? pythonExecutable;

        string[] allArgs = args is { Length: > 0 }
            ? ["run", scriptPath, .. args]
            : ["run", scriptPath];

        var projectResource = new UvAppResource(name,
projectDirectory);

        var resourceBuilder = builder.
AddResource(projectResource)
            .WithArgs(allArgs)
            .WithArgs(context =>
            {
                // If the project is to be automatically
instrumented, add the instrumentation executable
arguments first.
                if (!string.
```

```
IsNullOrEmpty(instrumentationExecutable))
            {
                    AddOpenTelemetryArguments(context);

                    // // Add the python executable as
the next argument so we can run the project.
                    // context.Args.
Add(pythonExecutable!);
            }
        });

        if (!string.
IsNullOrEmpty(instrumentationExecutable))
        {
            resourceBuilder.WithOtlpExporter();

            // Make sure to attach the logging
instrumentation setting, so we can capture logs.
            // Without this you'll need to configure
logging yourself. Which is kind of a pain.
            resourceBuilder.WithEnvironment("OTEL_PYTHON_
LOGGING_AUTO_INSTRUMENTATION_ENABLED", "true");
        }

        return resourceBuilder;
    }

    private static void
AddOpenTelemetryArguments(CommandLineArgsCallbackContext
context)
    {
        context.Args.Add("--traces_exporter");
        context.Args.Add("otlp");

        context.Args.Add("--logs_exporter");
        context.Args.Add("console,otlp");

        context.Args.Add("--metrics_exporter");
        context.Args.Add("otlp");
    }
```

Note that for each of these languages, we are missing a few details: the way they need to be published and the **WithHttpEndpoint** method. This is a conscious choice: since those are two extension methods that require actual configuration by the developer (Where is the Dockerfile located? What is the port your web service is listening on? Should it be proxied?), it would not make sense to receive all this information in the **AddGolangApp** method.

Another thing the developer needs to take care of when dealing with other languages is the need to instrument their application with OpenTelemetry. The **WithOtlpExporter()** method will simply inject the environment variables needed to connect to the OpenTelemetry endpoint provided by .NET Aspire. When we add a .NET project, the actual instrumentation is handled by the **ServiceDefaults** project, as discussed in the previous chapters. Of course, we cannot use those .NET extension methods in a Golang application.

Lastly, service discovery is different now. While .NET natively supports service discovery to automatically create an HTTP client based on the environment variable injected by .NET Aspire, this is not true for other languages. However, we can still use those environment variables freely when we need to call other services via http. An example can be seen in the Golang code:

```
req, err := http.NewRequest("POST", os.Getenv("services__
dab__http__0")+"/api/Orders", strings.
NewReader(string(reqBody)))
        if err != nil {
            c.JSON(http.StatusInternalServerError,
gin.H{"error": "Failed to create request"})
            return
        }
```

Conclusion

In this chapter, we explored the power and flexibility of .NET Aspire in orchestrating polyglot microservice architectures. We have shown how to leverage the strengths of each language by writing services in Go, Python, and Node.js and extensions to support. With the help of the .NET Aspire Community Toolkit, we were able to streamline integration with .NET Aspire. We examined how .NET Aspire helps in service discovery and OpenTelemetry integration across languages.

By understanding these nuances, developers can build and manage complex, multi-language microservice applications.

Finally, this chapter empowers developers with knowledge and practical skills to harness the full potential of .NET Aspire in truly creating robust distributed systems by choosing the best tools for each component and achieving good results.

In the next chapter, we will discuss .NET Aspire monitoring and health checks.

Join our Discord space

Join our Discord workspace for latest updates, offers, tech happenings around the world, new releases, and sessions with the authors:

https://discord.bpbonline.com

CHAPTER 4
.NET Aspire Monitoring

Introduction

In the previous chapters, we focused mainly on building our e-commerce application as a collection of microservices leveraging different frameworks. However, it is crucial to ensure we maintain the health, performance, and reliability of our distributed system to operate. This chapter explores the key aspects of .NET Aspire monitoring and observability by providing the necessary tools and techniques to help you learn insights about the distributed application's behavior and to identify and resolve any issues.

Structure

In this chapter, we will discuss the following topics:

- Monitoring in cloud-native applications
- OpenTelemetry fundamentals
- Benefits of OpenTelemetry

- Instrumenting a .NET Aspire application with OpenTelementry
- Analyzing and visualizing Telemetry

Objectives

The primary objective of this chapter is to provide readers with an understanding of monitoring in .NET Aspire applications. By the end of the chapter, you will learn about the importance of monitoring and observability, explore built-in features for collecting logs and metrics, integrate with other popular monitoring tools, and implement distributed tracing to gain insights about requests. This knowledge will help you to debug your application and look for any performance bottlenecks.

Monitoring in cloud-native applications

In today's fast-paced world of building cloud native microservice applications, monitoring is a critical component in ensuring these services operate efficiently and reliably. These applications are designed to be highly scalable and leverage modern technologies like containers, serverless computing, etc., which introduces challenges in understanding system behavior and identifying potential issues. These applications are often designed in a distributed nature, consisting of multiple microservices communicating with each other, which causes difficulties in tracking interactions between them. Monitoring helps in managing this complexity by providing a clear picture of how different components communicate and interact with each other.

Key benefits of monitoring

The following are the key benefits of monitoring:

- **Early detection**: Monitoring allows you to catch anomalies, errors, or performance issues early. This timely detection enables you to intervene and prevent services from disruptions, data loss, or security breaches. By identifying early issues before they escalate, we can ensure systems remain stable and secure.

- **Performance optimization**: Through monitoring, you can track key performance metrics to identify areas where optimization is needed. This leads to improved efficiency, resource utilization, and overall system responsiveness.

- **Capacity planning**: Monitoring provides insights into resource usage trends, aiding in capacity planning and forecasting. By understanding how resources are being used, we can ensure that the system is better prepared to handle future growth and demand.

- **Security enhancement**: Monitoring helps detect suspicious activity or unauthorized access attempts, which helps in enhancing the overall security of the system.

- **Root cause analysis**: In the event of an incident, monitoring data can be used to perform a root cause analysis, identify the underlying cause of the problem, and prevent it from happening.

- **Compliance and auditing**: Monitoring can help ensure compliance with regulatory requirements and internal policies by providing auditable records of system activity.

- **Improving user experience**: By monitoring user interactions and application performance, organizations can identify and address issues that impact the user experience.

Overall, monitoring is essential for maintaining the reliability, availability, and performance of any system or application. By leveraging monitoring, organizations can build highly available, robust, efficient, and user-friendly systems.

Observability

Observability is the ability to understand the internal state of a system by collecting and examining its telemetry data. For example, imagine you are driving a car, and the dashboard shows you details about speed, gas level, engine temperature, etc., which are basic monitoring metrics. However, observability is like turning this into a smart car, which not only shows basic details but can also tell you when any of the car components are failing and how it affects other parts of the car. Instead of just knowing our system is not working properly, observability will give us complete details and insights to help us understand what is wrong and what we need to do to make it right. In simple terms, monitoring tells you when a known problem occurs (when is the *check engine* light is on) and observability gives you the tools to investigate the unknown problems (the ability to query logs, traces and metrics to find out why the light is on). OpenTelemetry is an industry standard to achieve this goal.

OpenTelemetry fundamentals

OpenTelemetry is a **Cloud Native Computing Foundation (CNCF)** and an open source and vendor-neutral Observability framework that is supported by major cloud providers for instrumenting, generating, collecting, and exporting telemetry data (metrics, logs, and traces) to help you analyze your software's performance and behavior. OpenTelemetry is a collection of **application programming interface (APIs)**, **software development kits (SDKs)**, and tools: for more details, refer to OpenTelemetry's official documentation at **https://opentelemetry.io/**. OpenTelemetry mainly focuses on three main types of telemetry data:

- **Traces**: Traces stores the execution of a request and helps in tracking the request flow inside a distributed system. They help in understanding the end-to-end journey of any request traveling across multiple services within a distributed system.

- **Metrics**: Metrics are often collected at regular intervals and are numerical measurements that help in providing insights into the application's health and performance.

- **Logs**: Logs are the primary way to collect telemetry data. Logs are time-stamped based records that track all the events that happened over time. They are crucial in debugging and understanding system behavior. When properly structured, logs can be enriched with many dimensions that allow for powerful filtering and correlation.

While each of these data types provides valuable insights on their own, however, when they are combined together, they can provide a complete understanding of the application's behavior, which helps in identifying the root cause of problems and optimizing application performance.

Benefits of OpenTelemetry

OpenTelemetry has become a game changer in the world of application monitoring and observability due to the following benefits:

- **Vendor flexibility**: OpenTelemetry provides the flexibility to change backends without having to change instrumentation code, which prevents vendor lock-in and gives you the freedom to select tools based on your application needs.

- **Supports multiple languages and frameworks**: OpenTelemetry provides a single set of standards that helps in supporting multiple languages and integrates with most popular frameworks.

- **Streamlined telemetry data management**: OpenTelemetry simplifies the process of managing and exporting telemetry data, which helps in dealing with the complexities of observability in distributed systems.

- **Standardization and interoperability**: OpenTelemetry establishes a standardized format and protocol for telemetry data that promotes interoperability between different observability tools and systems.

- **Community driven and open source**: OpenTelemetry benefits from a large active open source community, which fosters collaboration and innovation. The open-source nature ensures transparency and encourages contributions.

OpenTelemetry components

OpenTelemetry consists of the following components:

- **API**: Defines data types and operations for generating and correlating tracing, metrics, and logging data.

- **SDK**: Language-specific implementation of the OpenTelemetry API.

- **Collector**: It provides a vendor-agnostic implementation for receiving, processing, and exporting telemetry data. It consists of the following three components:

o **Receiver**: To receive telemetry data in multiple formats, like **OpenTelemetry Line Protocol (OTLP)** and from open-source systems like Jaeger and Prometheus.

o **Processor**: To process telemetry data (log, trace, and metric).

o **Exporter**: To send data to the backend.

OpenTelemetry instrumentation

Instrumentation is nothing but emitting telemetry data (log, metrics, traces) from system components to observe its performance and health. You can use either or both code based and zero code solutions to instrument. OpenTelemetry code instrumentation is supported for many different programming languages, and you can find the complete list on the official documentation at **https://opentelemetry. io/docs/languages/#status-and-releases**.

Instrumenting .NET Aspire applications with OpenTelemetry

We will utilize code-based solutions (via SDKs) to see how to integrate open telemetry with .NET Aspire applications to instrument telemetry data. For this chapter, we will consider how to set up OpenTelemetry inside **WarehouseAPI** (.NET backend API project), which includes configuring OpenTelemetry to collect telemetry data and then using exporters to send it to various backends.

Setting up OpenTelemetry inside WarehouseAPI project

The .NET Aspire project provides a convenient way to set up OpenTelemetry through its built-in service defaults. This setup ensures that all necessary components for monitoring and observability are configured correctly with minimal effort.

You can observe inside the `Eshop.ServiceDefaults` project, the following OpenTelemetry .NET NuGet packages were added by default when you set up the project:

```
<PackageReference Include="OpenTelemetry.Exporter.
OpenTelemetryProtocol" />
<PackageReference Include="OpenTelemetry.Extensions.
Hosting" />
<PackageReference Include="OpenTelemetry.Instrumentation.
AspNetCore" />
<PackageReference Include="OpenTelemetry.Instrumentation.
Http" />
<PackageReference Include="OpenTelemetry.Instrumentation.
Runtime" />
```

These are needed for configuring OpenTelemetry inside the .NET Aspire application:

- **Adding service defaults**: The **AddServiceDefaults** method in the **Extensions.cs** class inside **Eshop.ServiceDefaults** project is the main entry point for configuring OpenTelemetry. This method is called from the **Program.cs** file during application startup, as shown in the following codes:

```
var builder = WebApplication.CreateBuilder(args);


// Add service defaults & Aspire components.
builder.AddServiceDefaults();
```

The **AddServiceDefaults** method configures several other services, such as health checks, service discovery, and resilience, as shown in the following:

```
public static IHostApplicationBuilder
AddServiceDefaults(this IHostApplicationBuilder
builder)
{
    builder.ConfigureOpenTelemetry();

    builder.AddDefaultHealthChecks();

    builder.Services.AddServiceDiscovery();

    builder.Services.
ConfigureHttpClientDefaults(http =>
    {
        // Turn on resilience by default
```

```
        http.AddStandardResilienceHandler();

        // Turn on service discovery by default
        http.AddServiceDiscovery();
    });

    return builder;
}
```

The **ConfigureOpenTelemetry** method is an extension method for the **IHostApplicationBuilder** interface and is responsible for setting up OpenTelemetry logging, metrics, and tracing. Let us take a look at how to configure logging, metrics, and traces inside this method.

- **Logging**: OpenTelemetry logging is configured to include formatted messages and scopes, which provide additional context for log entries:

```
builder.Logging.AddOpenTelemetry(logging =>
{
    logging.IncludeFormattedMessage = true;
    logging.IncludeScopes = true;
});
```

- **Metrics**: Metrics are configured to include instrumentation for ASP.NET Core, HTTP clients, and the runtime. This configuration makes sure that the KPIs are collected from various parts of the application:

```
builder.Services.AddOpenTelemetry()
    .WithMetrics(metrics =>
    {
        metrics.AddAspNetCoreInstrumentation()
            .AddHttpClientInstrumentation()
            .AddRuntimeInstrumentation();
    });
```

Details about these extension methods are as follows:

- o **AddAspNetCoreInstrumentation**: This instrumentation collects metrics related to ASP.NET Core requests, such as request duration and response status codes.

- o **AddHttpClientInstrumentation**: This instrumentation collects metrics related to HTTP client requests, such as request duration and response status codes.

- o **AddRuntimeInstrumentation**: This instrumentation collects metrics related to the .NET runtime, such as garbage collection and thread pool usage.

- **Tracing**: Tracing is configured to include instrumentation for ASP.NET Core and HTTP clients, just like how we configured metrics. This configuration allows us to trace incoming and outgoing requests and responses across different services and components:

```
builder.Services.AddOpenTelemetry()
    .WithTracing(tracing =>
    {
        tracing.AddAspNetCoreInstrumentation()
            .AddHttpClientInstrumentation();
    });
```

The complete method details are shown in the following, combining all the telemetry data configuration:

```
public static IHostApplicationBuilder
ConfigureOpenTelemetry(this IHostApplicationBuilder
builder)
    {
        builder.Logging.AddOpenTelemetry(logging =>
        {
            logging.IncludeFormattedMessage = true;
            logging.IncludeScopes = true;
        });

        builder.Services.AddOpenTelemetry()
            .WithMetrics(metrics =>
            {
                metrics.AddAspNetCoreInstrumentation()
                    .AddHttpClientInstrumentation()
                    .AddRuntimeInstrumentation();
            })
            .WithTracing(tracing =>
            {
```

```
                    tracing.AddAspNetCoreInstrumentation()
                    // Uncomment the following
line to enable gRPC instrumentation (requires
the OpenTelemetry.Instrumentation.GrpcNetClient
package)
                    //.AddGrpcClientInstrumentation()
                    .AddHttpClientInstrumentation();
        });

    builder.AddOpenTelemetryExporters();

    return builder;
}
```

Note: **Instead of exporting to the dashboard (OLTP), we can export to the console by adding the AddConsoleExporter method from OpenTelemetry .NET SDK. We can configure it on logging, metrics, or tracing configuration, which allows developers to output telemetry data directly to the console window. This is mainly useful during development and debugging phases when you want to visualize the telemetry data that your application is generating quickly, and it is not recommended for production.**

- **Exporting Telemetry data:** The **AddOpenTelemetryExporters** method configures the exporters for telemetry data. Exporters are responsible for sending collected telemetry data to various backends, such as OpenTelemetry Collector Azure Monitor, Jaeger, or Prometheus:

```
private static IHostApplicationBuilder
AddOpenTelemetryExporters(this
IHostApplicationBuilder builder)
{
    var useOtlpExporter = !string.
IsNullOrWhiteSpace(builder.Configuration["OTEL_
EXPORTER_OTLP_ENDPOINT"]);

    if (useOtlpExporter)
    {
        builder.Services.AddOpenTelemetry().
UseOtlpExporter();
```

```
        }

        return builder;
    }
```

In the above method, the OLTP exporter is configured if the **OTEL_ EXPORTER_OTLP_ENDPOINT** configuration setting was provided. This exporter then sends telemetry data to an OpenTelemetry Collector endpoint.

Similarly, in order to enable Azure Monitor Exporter, you can add the following code inside the **AddOpenTelemetryExporters** method:

```
if(!string.IsNullOrEmpty(builder.
Configuration["APPLICATIONINSIGHTS_CONNECTION_STRING"]))
{
    builder.Services.AddOpenTelemetry()
        .UseAzureMonitor();
}
```

Health checks in .NET Aspire

Health checks in .NET Aspire are key components in maintaining the reliability and availability of applications. Health checks make sure your application is responsive and capable of handling requests. These checks mainly provide information about the application's state, which helps in identifying any potential issues before they impact the business users.

Let us look at how to implement health checks in our Eshop application for monitoring the health of the application and also to expose endpoints that can be queries to check applications' health. Inside any .NET Aspire application, health checks are primarily configured in the **Extensions.cs** file within the **ServiceDefaults** project.

The **AddDefaultHealthChecks** method sets up basic health checks for the application. It adds a default health check named self, which always returns a healthy status. The health check is tagged with live to indicate it is a liveness check, as shown as follows:

```
public static IHostApplicationBuilder
AddDefaultHealthChecks(this IHostApplicationBuilder
```

```
builder)
{
    builder.Services.AddHealthChecks()
        // Add a default liveness check to ensure app is
responsive
        .AddCheck("self", () => HealthCheckResult.
Healthy(), ["live"]);

    return builder;
}
```

Inside the **Program.cs** file, health checks endpoints are mapped to specific routes, allowing the monitoring of the health of the application:

app.MapDefaultEndpoints();

The **MapDefaultEndpoints** method maps the health check endpoints to the application's HTTP pipeline. In a development environment, this method maps two endpoints:

- **/health**: All health checks must pass for the application to be considered as ready
- **/alive**: Only health checks that are tagged with **live** must pass for the application to be considered ready.

The complete method details are shown in the following:

```
public static WebApplication MapDefaultEndpoints(this
WebApplication app)
{
    if (app.Environment.IsDevelopment())
    {
        app.MapHealthChecks("/health");
        app.MapHealthChecks("/alive", new
HealthCheckOptions
        {
            Predicate = r => r.Tags.Contains("live")
        });
    }

    return app;
}
```

Inside the WarehouseAPI project, the health checks are integrated as part of the service defaults in the **Program.cs** file by calling the **MapDefaultEndpoints** method as shown in the following:

```
app.MapDefaultEndpoints();
```

Analyzing and visualizing Telemetry

Let us run our Eshop .NET Aspire application directly from Visual Studio. The Aspire dashboard is accessible at **https://localhost:17136/** which is printed on the console logs as shown in *Figure 4.1* along with the token:

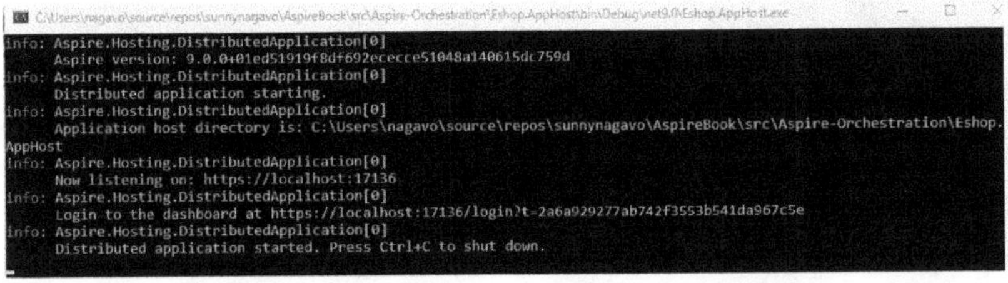

Figure 4.1: Console logs window with Aspire dashboard URL details

Once you open the URL in any browser, it will display the default resources tab view where you can see the health state of various services inside your .NET Aspire application, as shown in *Figure 4.2*. There is also an option to stop or restart any individual service directly from the dashboard under **Actions** column:

Figure 4.2: .NET Aspire dashboard with resources view

On the left-hand side, you can see tabs related to telemetry data (logs, metrics, and traces) emitted by different services within your application.

Click on the **Structured** tab, where you can view both system logs and log messages written inside your controllers. There is a drop-down at the top to filter based on different resources, as shown in *Figure 4.3*:

Figure 4.3: *Structured logs view for warehouseapi resource*

You can click on any specific trace to get more details about the request and its dependency, as shown in *Figure 4.4*. It displays GET requests for **/api/warehousestatus** endpoint, which internally calls the DAB container to retrieve information. The trace clearly shows the **warehouseapi** service making calls to the DAB service:

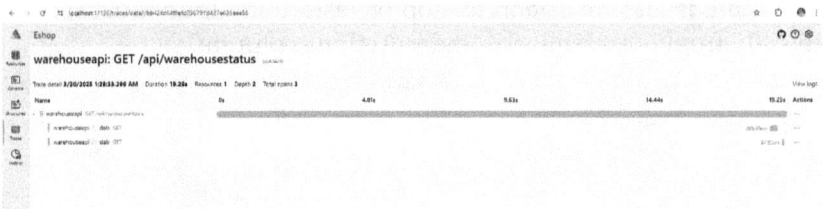

Figure 4.4: *Trace view for a particular trace request hitting /api/warehousestatus endpoint*

You can also see all trace requests within your application by navigating to the **Traces** tab and selecting the appropriate resource on the dashboard, as shown in *Figure 4.5*:

Figure 4.5: Displays list of all traces in traces view

The trace page view displays timestamp, name, spans, and duration, which helps in capturing enough details for analyzing the request, which is helpful during debugging.

Clicking on **Actions** and **View details** will give us more information about the request logs, as shown in *Figure 4.6*. This demonstrates the power of correlated telemetry, allowing you to pivot from a high-level trace directly to the detailed logs generated during that specific request.

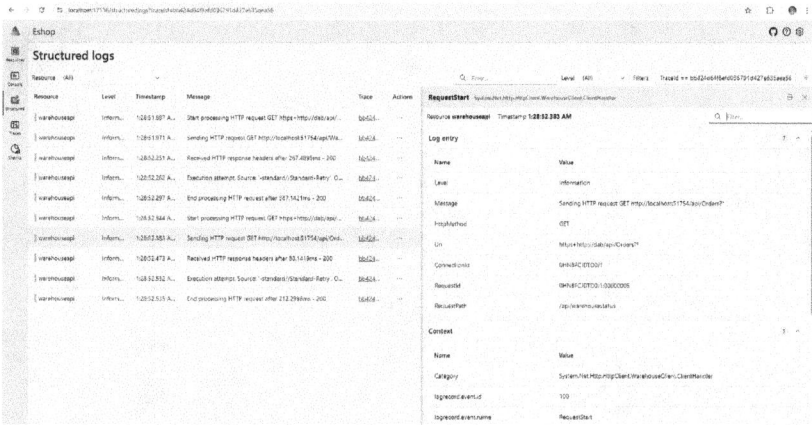

Figure 4.6: Details about RequestStart and log entries for a particular trace id

Click on the **Metrics** tab to display the **Metrics** view, which captures all the default metrics for all the resources within your application, as shown in *Figure 4.7*:

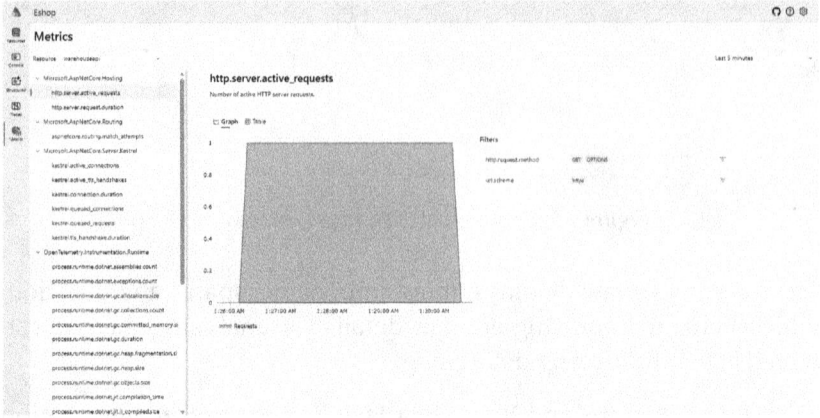

Figure 4.7: *Metrics view capturing default metrics*

Figure 4.8 displays one example of displaying HTTP request duration metrics for the **warehouseapi** service in graphical format:

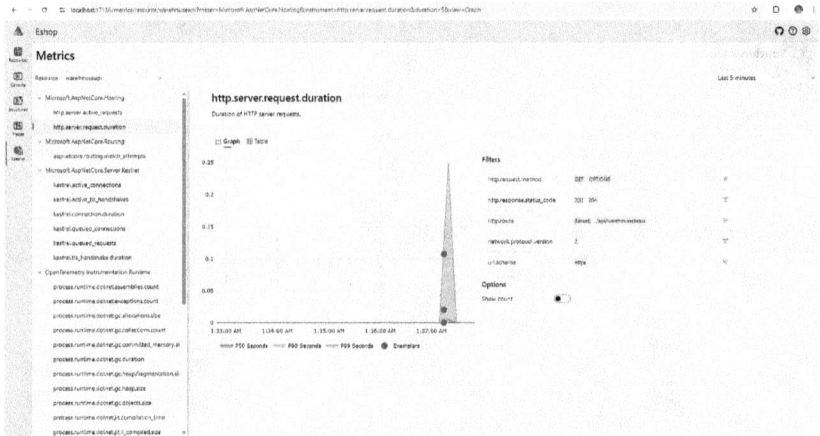

Figure 4.8: *HTTP server request duration metrics view*

Metrics page also includes the option to view the data in table format, as shown in *Figure 4.9*:

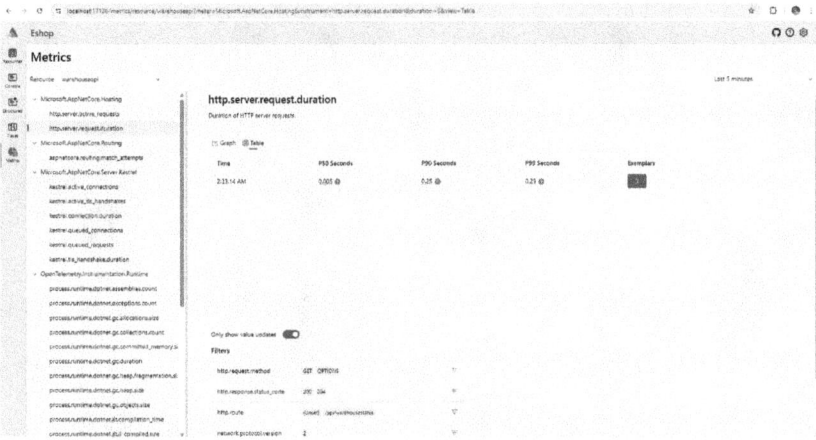

Figure 4.9: Table format displaying HTTP server request duration details

Conclusion

In this chapter, we explored the key role of monitoring and observability in .NET Aspire applications, particularly for maintaining the health, performance, and reliability of distributed systems. We explored the benefits of monitoring, the concept of observability, and the OpenTelemetry framework for generating, collecting, and exporting telemetry data.

We discussed how to set up OpenTelemetry using built-in service defaults, configure logging, metrics, and tracing, and export data to backends like OpenTelemetry Collector and Azure Monitor. Additionally, we covered health checks in .NET Aspire and the use of the .NET Aspire dashboard for analyzing and visualizing telemetry data. This chapter equips readers with the knowledge to effectively monitor .NET Aspire applications, optimize performance, and ensure the overall robustness of their distributed systems.

In the next chapter, we will explore how to deploy the application using azd tool.

Join our Discord space

Join our Discord workspace for latest updates, offers, tech happenings around the world, new releases, and sessions with the authors:

https://discord.bpbonline.com

CHAPTER 5

Deployments Using azd

Introduction

.NET Aspire is a great tool to help you debug your distributed applications locally. However, the hustle of building distributed applications does not stop at local debugging. When it comes to deploying these applications, it is not always as easy as it seems to make sure that everything is configured correctly. By leveraging the capabilities of **Azure Developer CLI (azd)**, developers can automate provisioning, configuration, and deployment of code and improve the deployment experience. In this chapter, we will see how .NET Aspire can work with the azd to make sure the deployment goes as smoothly as possible.

Structure

In this chapter, we will discuss the following topics:

- Introduction to azd and its benefits
- Installation and configuration of azd

- Use azd with .NET Aspire

- Development and deployment of Eshop application using azd

- Advanced azd features

Objectives

The primary objective of this chapter is to provide a comprehensive understanding of the azd and its use in application deployments to Azure. It covers the installation and configuration of azd, using it with sample templates to provision infrastructure and deploy code, and its interaction with .NET Aspire applications and manifests, including deployments using **azd up** and managing environment variables. The chapter also explains how azd dynamically generates Bicep files for infrastructure provisioning, facilitates transitions between different resource types, and applies these concepts to deploying a complex multi-language, multi-service distributed application. Additionally, it explored advanced features like setting up a CI/CD pipeline using azd for GitHub and pipeline configuration.

Introduction to azd and its benefits

You might already be familiar with the Azure CLI, which you can invoke with the **az** command. This CLI lets you handle standard commands to interact with basic Azure APIs. Using the Azure CLI, you can create and update resources.

The azd is invoked using the **azd** command. This CLI does not directly interact with Azure basic APIs. Rather, it is a CLI dedicated to developers who want to deploy their applications to Azure.

azd can either get you started when developing an application, offering you a template, or it can scan your current folder and match what is inside to one of its own templates. Once the code is matched to a template, you can use one command to provision the entire infrastructure needed to host your application and deploy your code on that infrastructure. The single command needed for this workflow is **azd up**, which will run two separate commands: **azd**

provision to provision the infrastructure and **azd deploy** to deploy the code. The **azd provision** command will use Bicep files to create the infrastructure.

Bicep is a domain-specific language that uses declarative syntax to deploy Azure resources. In a Bicep file, you define the infrastructure you want to deploy to Azure and then use that file throughout the development lifecycle to repeatedly deploy that infrastructure. Your resources are deployed in a consistent manner, thus implementing **infrastructure as code** (IaC). Natively, Azure infrastructures are described and deployed using **Azure Resource Manager** (ARM) templates. ARM templates are Json files and can be translated to Bicep files.

Here is an ARM JSON file to deploy an Azure Storage Account:

```json
{
  "$schema": "https://schema.management.azure.com/
schemas/2019-04-01/deploymentTemplate.json#",
  "contentVersion": "1.0.0.0",
  "parameters": {
    "location": {
      "type": "string",
      "defaultValue": "[resourceGroup().location]"
    },
    "storageAccountName": {
      "type": "string",
      "defaultValue": "[format('toylaunch{0}',
uniqueString(resourceGroup().id))]"
    }
  },
  "resources": [
    {
      "type": "Microsoft.Storage/storageAccounts",
      "apiVersion": "2023-05-01",
      "name": "[parameters('storageAccountName')]",
      "location": "[parameters('location')]",
      "sku": {
        "name": "Standard_LRS"
      },
      "kind": "StorageV2",
      "properties": {
```

```
      "accessTier": "Hot"
    }
  }
 ]
}
```

Here is the equivalent Bicep code:

```
param location string = resourceGroup().location
param storageAccountName string =
'toylaunch${uniqueString(resourceGroup().id)}'

resource storageAccount 'Microsoft.Storage/
storageAccounts@2023-05-01' = {
  name: storageAccountName
  location: location
  sku: {
    name: 'Standard_LRS'
  }
  kind: 'StorageV2'
  properties: {
    accessTier: 'Hot'
  }
}
```

Installation and configuration of azd

To start using azd, we need to install it. There are many ways to install the Azure Developer CLI. In this chapter, we will use **winget**, a tool to install, upgrade, and remove applications on Windows 10 and Windows 11. If you cannot use **winget**, we recommend visiting the official azd documentation (**https://learn.microsoft.com/en-us/ azure/developer/azure-developer-cli/overview?tabs=windows**) for other installation options.

Run the command below inside a terminal window:

winget install microsoft.azd

This will also install the GitHub CLI and the Bicep CLI. Verify the installation was successful by running:

azd version

Once the azd is installed, we can test one of its default templates to see how it works.

Open a terminal in a new empty folder and run this command:

```
azd init --template todo-nodejs-mongo
```

This will prompt the **azd** to create a new repository based on a known template. The code for this application will be downloaded from the template repository.

The CLI is now asking to enter an environment name. The environment represents a deployment environment. A folder with the environment name will be created under the **.azure** folder. Inside, we will find an **.env** file containing all the information regarding this specific deployment environment: Azure subscription ID, resource names, etc.

Enter the value **dev** and hit *Enter*.

Open the folder to look at the structure of this template:

```
- root
  - .azdo
    - pipelines
      - azure-dev.yml
  - .azure
    - config.json
  - .devcontainer
    - devcontainer.json
  - .github
    - workflows
  - .vscode
    - extensions.json
    - launch.json
    - tasks.json
  - assets
    - resources-with-apim.png
    - resources.png
    - urls.png
    - web.png
  - infra
```

```
      - abbreviations.json
      - main.bicep
      - main.parameters.json
      - app
      - core
  - src
    - api
    - web
  - tests
    - .gitignore
    - package.json
    - playwright.config.ts
    - README.md
    - todo.spec.ts
  - .gitattributes
  - .gitignore
  - azure.yaml
  - LICENSE
  - NOTICE.txt
  - openapi.yaml
  - README.md
```

The **src, assets**, and **test** folders contain specific files for the code of this application.

The **.azdo** folder contains the definition of an Azure DevOps Pipeline that will provision the infrastructure and deploy the code. The same pipeline definition can also be found in the **.github/workflows** folder. This will define a GitHub Action.

The **.azure** folder, as previously mentioned, contains a **dev** folder. The name matches the environment name we have defined during the repository initialization. In the **.env** file, we now only have a single environment variable:

```
AZURE_ENV_NAME="dev"
```

This variable will be set as a tag in each resource that will be deployed. This file will also be populated with further environment variables needed for the deployment of our application.

The **devcontainer** folder contains the definition of the container to run this application in a local **devcontainer**.

The **.vscode** folder contains specific launch settings to debug the application itself.

In the **infra** folder, there are the necessary Bicep files needed to provision this infrastructure.

Lastly, we can look at the **azure.yaml** file that contains specific instructions for the azd to determine where each code folder should be deployed:

```
# yaml-language-server: $schema=https://raw.
githubusercontent.com/Azure/azure-dev/main/schemas/v1.0/
azure.yaml.json

name: todo-nodejs-mongo
metadata:
  template: todo-nodejs-mongo@0.0.1-beta
workflows:
  up:
    steps:
      - azd: provision
      - azd: deploy --all
services:
  web:
    project: ./src/web
    dist: dist
    language: js
    host: appservice
    hooks:
      # Creates a temporary `.env.local` file for the
build command. Vite will automatically use it during
build.
      # The expected/required values are mapped to the
infrastructure outputs.
      # .env.local is ignored by git, so it will not be
committed if, for any reason, if deployment fails.
      # see: https://vitejs.dev/guide/env-and-mode
```

```
    # Note: Notice that dotenv must be a project
dependency for this to work. See package.json.
        prepackage:
          windows:
            shell: pwsh
            run: 'echo "VITE_API_BASE_URL=""$env:API_BASE_
URL""" > .env.local ; echo "VITE_APPLICATIONINSIGHTS_
CONNECTION_STRING=""$env:APPLICATIONINSIGHTS_CONNECTION_
STRING""" >> .env.local'
          posix:
            shell: sh
            run: 'echo VITE_API_BASE_URL=\"$API_BASE_URL\"
> .env.local && echo VITE_APPLICATIONINSIGHTS_CONNECTION_
STRING=\"$APPLICATIONINSIGHTS_CONNECTION_STRING\" >>
.env.local'
        postdeploy:
          windows:
            shell: pwsh
            run: 'rm .env.local'
          posix:
            shell: sh
            run: 'rm .env.local'
  api:
    project: ./src/api
    language: js
    host: appservice
```

Looking at the pipelines that this template has created, we can see that both perform two specific steps: **azd provision** and **azd deploy**. **azd provision** will use the **infra** folder to determine which Azure resources to deploy. **azd deploy** will use the **azure.yaml** file to determine how to deploy the code.

We have already described how the **azd up** command will invoke these two commands, one after the other. When it comes to automation pipelines, it makes sense to use the specific steps.

Use azd with .NET Aspire

The other use case of azd is when we have an already defined application and we want to use it to quickly deploy it to Azure. Our application needs to be mapped to one of the azd templates.

This is not always easy, because a distributed application can be composed with many different components. .NET Aspire works well with the azd, because it can describe the architecture of its own application with a manifest. That manifest can be analyzed by the azd to dynamically determine which resources it needs to deploy. When it comes to code deployment, a decision has been made: deploy every non-Azure resource as a container hosted in an Azure Container App.

Azure Container App is a serverless Azure resource based on Kubernetes. It can host microservices and containerized applications.

To better understand how azd and .NET Aspire can work together, we will use one of the .NET Aspire templates.

Open a terminal in an empty folder and run this command:

```
dotnet new aspire-starter --use-redis-cache
```

This will create a .NET Aspire application with a Blazor frontend, a .NET minimal API, and a Redis cache:

```
var builder = DistributedApplication.CreateBuilder(args);

var cache = builder.AddRedis("cache");

var apiService = builder.AddProject<Projects.test_
ApiService>("apiservice");

builder.AddProject<Projects.test_Web>("webfrontend")
    .WithExternalHttpEndpoints()
    .WithReference(cache)
    .WaitFor(cache)
    .WithReference(apiService)
    .WaitFor(apiService);

builder.Build().Run();
```

In the same terminal, run the command to initialize an azd environment:

```
azd init
```

> Note: **We are not specifying any template, because we want the azd to match our code to one of its own known templates. The CLI will prompt us to choose how to initialize our app. Choose the option Use the code in the current directory.**

You will see a message in the terminal that the CLI is scanning the folder. Once the scanning is complete, you should have an output like the following:

Output:

```
Detected services:

 .NET (Aspire)
 Detected in: D:\src\test\test.AppHost\test.AppHost.
csproj
```

azd will generate the files necessary to host your app on Azure using Azure Container Apps.

The terminal will now prompt to confirm and continue initializing my app. Press *Enter* and continue entering the environment name as we did in the previous example.

Since we are not initializing a template, we will not have the same folder structure we had before. azd has created for us only the environment folder under **.azure** and three files:

- **.gitignore**: The contents of this file are used to ignore files from git tracking, **.azure** folder is also added as it contains sensitive information such as the Azure subscription ID.

- **next-steps.md**: This is a Markdown file with instructions on the next steps to follow the azd initialization.

- **azure.yaml**: The **azure.yaml** file is different from the one we have seen in the previous example:

  ```
  #    yaml-language-server:    $schema=https://raw.
  githubusercontent.com/Azure/azure-dev/main/schemas/
  v1.0/azure.yaml.json
  ```

```
name: test
services:
  app:
    language: dotnet
    project: ./test.AppHost/test.AppHost.csproj
    host: containerapp
```

The only project considered here is the **AppHost**, as it is the entry point of the entire distributed application, and it can be described via the Aspire manifest, including all the different resources needed. You can see that the default host is **containerapp**.

There is no **infra** folder at this time. The infrastructure is not predefined, as the infrastructure of the application itself is dynamically defined in the **AppHost** project.

Every time we run **azd up**, the azd will run the command to build the **AppHost** project to get its manifest. You can do that on your own by running this command in the **AppHost** project folder:

dotnet run --publisher manifest --output-path ../aspire-manifest.json

A new file will be created in the root folder of our repository containing the JSON definition of the entire application:

```
{
    "$schema":    "https://json.schemastore.org/aspire-
8.0.json",
  "resources": {
    "cache": {
      "type": "container.v0",
      "connectionString": "{cache.bindings.tcp.host}:{cache.
bindings.tcp.port}",
      "image": "docker.io/library/redis:7.4",
      "bindings": {
        "tcp": {
          "scheme": "tcp",
          "protocol": "tcp",
          "transport": "tcp",
          "targetPort": 6379
```

```
        }
      }
    },
    "apiservice": {
      "type": "project.v0",
      "path": "test.ApiService/test.ApiService.csproj",
      "env": {
        "OTEL_DOTNET_EXPERIMENTAL_OTLP_EMIT_EXCEPTION_LOG_
ATTRIBUTES": "true",
            "OTEL_DOTNET_EXPERIMENTAL_OTLP_EMIT_EVENT_LOG_
ATTRIBUTES": "true",
        "OTEL_DOTNET_EXPERIMENTAL_OTLP_RETRY": "in_memory",
        "ASPNETCORE_FORWARDEDHEADERS_ENABLED": "true",
      "HTTP_PORTS": "{apiservice.bindings.http.targetPort}"
        },
      "bindings": {
        "http": {
          "scheme": "http",
          "protocol": "tcp",
          "transport": "http"
        },
        "https": {
          "scheme": "https",
          "protocol": "tcp",
          "transport": "http"
        }
      }
    },
    "webfrontend": {
      "type": "project.v0",
      "path": "test.Web/test.Web.csproj",
      "env": {
        "OTEL_DOTNET_EXPERIMENTAL_OTLP_EMIT_EXCEPTION_LOG_
ATTRIBUTES": "true",
            "OTEL_DOTNET_EXPERIMENTAL_OTLP_EMIT_EVENT_LOG_
ATTRIBUTES": "true",
        "OTEL_DOTNET_EXPERIMENTAL_OTLP_RETRY": "in_memory",
```

```
      "ASPNETCORE_FORWARDEDHEADERS_ENABLED": "true",
            "HTTP_PORTS":    "{webfrontend.bindings.http.
targetPort}",
    "ConnectionStrings__cache": "{cache.connectionString}",
          "services__apiservice__http__0": "{apiservice.
bindings.http.url}",
          "services__apiservice__https__0": "{apiservice.
bindings.https.url}"
      },
      "bindings": {
        "http": {
          "scheme": "http",
          "protocol": "tcp",
          "transport": "http",
          "external": true
        },
        "https": {
          "scheme": "https",
          "protocol": "tcp",
          "transport": "http",
          "external": true
        }
      }
    }
  }
}
```

The **cache** resource is of type **container.v0**. This means it will be deployed as a container. The **apiservice** and **webfronted** resources are of type **project.v0**. This resource type is a .NET project. .NET projects can be published as containers running the command:

```
dotnet publish --os linux --arch X64 /t:PublishContainer
```

So every time the azd finds a resource of type **project.v0**, it will run the command to publish that project as a container and deploy the resulting container image.

In this manifest, there are also the connection strings and environment variables needed by each resource. When deploying these different

Container Apps, the azd will configure the necessary values as instructed by the manifest.

The Bicep files to deploy the infrastructure will be dynamically generated and not written on disk. However, we can enable an experimental flag to create those files.

In the terminal, run the command below:

```
azd config set alpha.infraSynth on
```

This will enable the command **azd infra synth**. Run it in the root folder of our repository:

```
azd infra synth
```

This command will create two different **infra** folders. The first one contains the Bicep files and can be found under the root folder. The **main.bicep** file is the entry point of our IaC:

```
targetScope = 'subscription'


@minLength(1)
@maxLength(64)
@description('Name of the environment that can be used
as part of naming resource convention, the name of the
resource group for your application will use this name,
prefixed with rg-')
param environmentName string

@minLength(1)
@description('The location used for all deployed resources')
param location string

@description('Id of the user or app to assign application
roles')
param principalId string = ''



var tags = {
  'azd-env-name': environmentName
}
```

```
resource rg 'Microsoft.Resources/resourceGroups@2022-09-01'
= {
  name: 'rg-${environmentName}'
  location: location
  tags: tags
}

module resources 'resources.bicep' = {
  scope: rg
  name: 'resources'
  params: {
    location: location
    tags: tags
    principalId: principalId
  }
}

output  MANAGED_IDENTITY_CLIENT_ID  string  =  resources.
outputs.MANAGED_IDENTITY_CLIENT_ID
output  MANAGED_IDENTITY_NAME string = resources.outputs.
MANAGED_IDENTITY_NAME
output  AZURE_LOG_ANALYTICS_WORKSPACE_NAME  string  =
resources.outputs.AZURE_LOG_ANALYTICS_WORKSPACE_NAME
output  AZURE_CONTAINER_REGISTRY_ENDPOINT  string  =
resources.outputs.AZURE_CONTAINER_REGISTRY_ENDPOINT
output AZURE_CONTAINER_REGISTRY_MANAGED_IDENTITY_ID string
=    resources.outputs.AZURE_CONTAINER_REGISTRY_MANAGED_
IDENTITY_ID
output AZURE_CONTAINER_REGISTRY_NAME string = resources.
outputs.AZURE_CONTAINER_REGISTRY_NAME
output  AZURE_CONTAINER_APPS_ENVIRONMENT_NAME  string  =
resources.outputs.AZURE_CONTAINER_APPS_ENVIRONMENT_NAME
output  AZURE_CONTAINER_APPS_ENVIRONMENT_ID  string  =
resources.outputs.AZURE_CONTAINER_APPS_ENVIRONMENT_ID
output   AZURE_CONTAINER_APPS_ENVIRONMENT_DEFAULT_DOMAIN
string    =    resources.outputs.AZURE_CONTAINER_APPS_
ENVIRONMENT_DEFAULT_DOMAIN
```

This file will create the resource group and load the module **resources.bicep,** described in the **resources.bicep** file:

```
@description('The location used for all deployed resources')
param location string = resourceGroup().location
@description('Id of the user or app to assign application
roles')
param principalId string = ''


@description('Tags that will be applied to all resources')
param tags object = {}

var resourceToken = uniqueString(resourceGroup().id)

resource  managedIdentity  'Microsoft.ManagedIdentity/
userAssignedIdentities@2023-01-31' = {
  name: 'mi-${resourceToken}'
  location: location
  tags: tags
}

resource containerRegistry 'Microsoft.ContainerRegistry/
registries@2023-07-01' = {
  name: replace('acr-${resourceToken}', '-', '')
  location: location
  sku: {
    name: 'Basic'
  }
  tags: tags
}

resource caeMiRoleAssignment 'Microsoft.Authorization/
roleAssignments@2022-04-01' = {
    name: guid(containerRegistry.id, managedIdentity.
id,    subscriptionResourceId('Microsoft.Authorization/
roleDefinitions', '7f951dda-4ed3-4680-a7ca-43fe172d538d'))
  scope: containerRegistry
```

```
  properties: {
    principalId: managedIdentity.properties.principalId
    principalType: 'ServicePrincipal'
     roleDefinitionId:   subscriptionResourceId('Microsoft.
Authorization/roleDefinitions',    '7f951dda-4ed3-4680-a7ca-
43fe172d538d')
  }
}


resource        logAnalyticsWorkspace        'Microsoft.
OperationalInsights/workspaces@2022-10-01' = {
  name: 'law-${resourceToken}'
  location: location
  properties: {
    sku: {
      name: 'PerGB2018'
    }
  }
  tags: tags
}


resource      containerAppEnvironment      'Microsoft.App/
managedEnvironments@2024-02-02-preview' = {
  name: 'cae-${resourceToken}'
  location: location
  properties: {
    workloadProfiles: [{
      workloadProfileType: 'Consumption'
      name: 'consumption'
    }]
    appLogsConfiguration: {
      destination: 'log-analytics'
      logAnalyticsConfiguration: {
            customerId: logAnalyticsWorkspace.properties.
customerId
            sharedKey: logAnalyticsWorkspace.listKeys().
primarySharedKey
```

```
      }
    }
  }
  tags: tags

  resource aspireDashboard 'dotNetComponents' = {
    name: 'aspire-dashboard'
    properties: {
      componentType: 'AspireDashboard'
    }
  }


}

resource explicitContributorUserRoleAssignment 'Microsoft.
Authorization/roleAssignments@2022-04-01' = {
    name: guid(containerAppEnvironment.id, principalId,
subscriptionResourceId('Microsoft.Authorization/
roleDefinitions', 'b24988ac-6180-42a0-ab88-20f7382dd24c'))
  scope: containerAppEnvironment
  properties: {
    principalId: principalId
      roleDefinitionId: subscriptionResourceId('Microsoft.
Authorization/roleDefinitions', 'b24988ac-6180-42a0-ab88-
20f7382dd24c')
  }
}

output MANAGED_IDENTITY_CLIENT_ID string = managedIdentity.
properties.clientId
output MANAGED_IDENTITY_NAME string = managedIdentity.name
output      MANAGED_IDENTITY_PRINCIPAL_ID      string      =
managedIdentity.properties.principalId
output    AZURE_LOG_ANALYTICS_WORKSPACE_NAME    string    =
logAnalyticsWorkspace.name
output     AZURE_LOG_ANALYTICS_WORKSPACE_ID     string     =
logAnalyticsWorkspace.id
output     AZURE_CONTAINER_REGISTRY_ENDPOINT     string     =
```

```
containerRegistry.properties.loginServer
output AZURE_CONTAINER_REGISTRY_MANAGED_IDENTITY_ID string
= managedIdentity.id
output      AZURE_CONTAINER_REGISTRY_NAME      string      =
containerRegistry.name
output   AZURE_CONTAINER_APPS_ENVIRONMENT_NAME   string   =
containerAppEnvironment.name
output   AZURE_CONTAINER_APPS_ENVIRONMENT_ID   string   =
containerAppEnvironment.id
output      AZURE_CONTAINER_APPS_ENVIRONMENT_DEFAULT_DOMAIN
string = containerAppEnvironment.properties.defaultDomain
```

In here, we create the Azure Container Registry that will hold the custom Docker images of microservices, the Log Analytics Workspace to collect telemetry from our resources, and the authorization configuration using Azure Managed Identities. We also define the configuration for the Azure Container App Environment.

You can notice that there is no specific configuration for each of the Container Apps composing our application. Azure Container Apps are defined via YAML files in a similar way to Kubernetes deployment files.

These files can be found in the **infra** folder under the **AppHost** folder. In here, we can see three files:

- **apiservice.tmpl.yaml**
- **cache.tmpl.yaml**
- **webfrontend.tmpl.yaml**

Note: **Since we have not specified any specific cloud implementation of Redis, azd is provisioning Redis as a custom container.**

The **webfrontend.tmpl.yaml** will look like this:

```
api-version: 2024-02-02-preview
location: {{ .Env.AZURE_LOCATION }}
identity:
  type: UserAssigned
  userAssignedIdentities:
    ? "{{ .Env.AZURE_CONTAINER_REGISTRY_MANAGED_IDENTITY_
ID }}"
```

```
      : {}
properties:
  environmentId: {{ .Env.AZURE_CONTAINER_APPS_
ENVIRONMENT_ID }}
  configuration:
    activeRevisionsMode: single
    runtime:
      dotnet:
        autoConfigureDataProtection: true
    ingress:
      external: true
      targetPort: {{ targetPortOrDefault 8080 }}
      transport: http
      allowInsecure: false
    registries:
      - server: {{ .Env.AZURE_CONTAINER_REGISTRY_ENDPOINT
}}
        identity: {{ .Env.AZURE_CONTAINER_REGISTRY_
MANAGED_IDENTITY_ID }}
    secrets:
      - name: connectionstrings--cache
        value: cache:6379
  template:
    containers:
      - image: {{ .Image }}
        name: webfrontend
        env:
          - name: AZURE_CLIENT_ID
            value: {{ .Env.MANAGED_IDENTITY_CLIENT_ID }}
          - name: ASPNETCORE_FORWARDEDHEADERS_ENABLED
            value: "true"
          - name: HTTP_PORTS
            value: '{{ targetPortOrDefault 0 }}'
          - name: OTEL_DOTNET_EXPERIMENTAL_OTLP_EMIT_
EVENT_LOG_ATTRIBUTES
            value: "true"
          - name: OTEL_DOTNET_EXPERIMENTAL_OTLP_EMIT_
```

```
EXCEPTION_LOG_ATTRIBUTES
            value: "true"
          - name: OTEL_DOTNET_EXPERIMENTAL_OTLP_RETRY
            value: in_memory
          - name: services__apiservice__http__0
            value: http://apiservice.internal.{{ .Env.
AZURE_CONTAINER_APPS_ENVIRONMENT_DEFAULT_DOMAIN }}
          - name: services__apiservice__https__0
            value: https://apiservice.internal.{{ .Env.
AZURE_CONTAINER_APPS_ENVIRONMENT_DEFAULT_DOMAIN }}
          - name: ConnectionStrings__cache
            secretRef: connectionstrings--cache
      scale:
        minReplicas: 1
tags:
  azd-service-name: webfrontend
  aspire-resource-name: webfrontend
```

As you can see, all the environment variables defined in the .NET Aspire manifest have been reflected in this YAML file to automatically configure all these values at deployment time. Doing so, the value connection string of the Redis cache will match the URL of the dedicated Container App.

We have set the **webfrontend** resource with the **.WithExternalHttpEndpoint()** method in the AppHost:

```
builder.AddProject<Projects.test_Web>("webfrontend")
    .WithExternalHttpEndpoints()
    .WithReference(cache)
    .WaitFor(cache)
    .WithReference(apiService)
    .WaitFor(apiService);
```

Therefore, the Ingress definition for the Container App has been set to external:

```
    ingress:
      external: true
      targetPort: {{ targetPortOrDefault 8080 }}
      transport: http
```

```
    allowInsecure: false
```

Open the **cache.tmpl.yaml** and see that the Ingress is set to internal only:

```
api-version: 2024-02-02-preview
location: {{ .Env.AZURE_LOCATION }}
identity:
  type: UserAssigned
  userAssignedIdentities:
    ? "{{ .Env.AZURE_CONTAINER_REGISTRY_MANAGED_IDENTITY_
ID }}"
    : {}
properties:
  environmentId: {{ .Env.AZURE_CONTAINER_APPS_ENVIRONMENT_
ID }}
  configuration:
    activeRevisionsMode: single
    runtime:
      dotnet:
        autoConfigureDataProtection: true
    ingress:
      external: false
      targetPort: 6379
      transport: tcp
      allowInsecure: false
    registries:
      - server: {{ .Env.AZURE_CONTAINER_REGISTRY_ENDPOINT
}}
        identity: {{ .Env.AZURE_CONTAINER_REGISTRY_MANAGED_
IDENTITY_ID }}
  template:
    containers:
      - image: {{ .Image }}
        name: cache
        env:
          - name: AZURE_CLIENT_ID
            value: {{ .Env.MANAGED_IDENTITY_CLIENT_ID }}
    scale:
```

```
      minReplicas: 1
tags:
  azd-service-name: cache
  aspire-resource-name: cache
```

Since Azure Container App is based on Kubernetes, it provides, by default, a virtual network that will allow our microservices to talk to each other without exposing them to the internet. We can expose specific services as needed, as we did with the frontend.

We can now run the command to deploy everything on Azure. First, we need to log into Azure with the azd. Note that this is needed only the first time:

azd auth login

Then run the command below:

azd up

The CLI will ask to select an Azure Subscription and an Azure Location. Then it will start provisioning the resources and deploying the code afterwards. Note that while this command is running, the **.env** in the corresponding environment folder will be populated with more environment variables.

Once the deployment is done, you will see endpoints for each Container App as shown in *Figure 5.1*. The Aspire dashboard has also been enabled on the Container Apps Environment:

Type	Name	State	Start time	Source	Endpoints	Actions
Container	apiservice	⬤ Running	22/03/2025 19:58:22	acrvojenwgtlet3a.azurecr.io/test/apiservic...	https://apiservice.internal.thankfulmushro...	■ ⬚ ...
Container	cache	⬤ Running	22/03/2025 19:58:39	docker.io/library/redis:7.4	https://cache.internal.thankfulmushroom-...	■ ⬚ ...
Container	webfrontend	⬤ Running	22/03/2025 19:39:14	acrvojenwgtlet3a.azurecr.io/test/webfront...	https://webfrontend.thankfulmushroom-6...	■ ⬚ ...

Figure 5.1: .NET Aspire dashboard with list of deployed resources

Note: The dashboard features are the same as the local one, except all resources are now containers, and the endpoints are not localhost. Also, cache and apiservice are marked as internal, as you can see from the endpoint which contains the .internal. Therefore, you would not be able to reach those resources from your browser.

On the Azure portal, you should see the list of all deployed resources as shown in *Figure 5.2*:

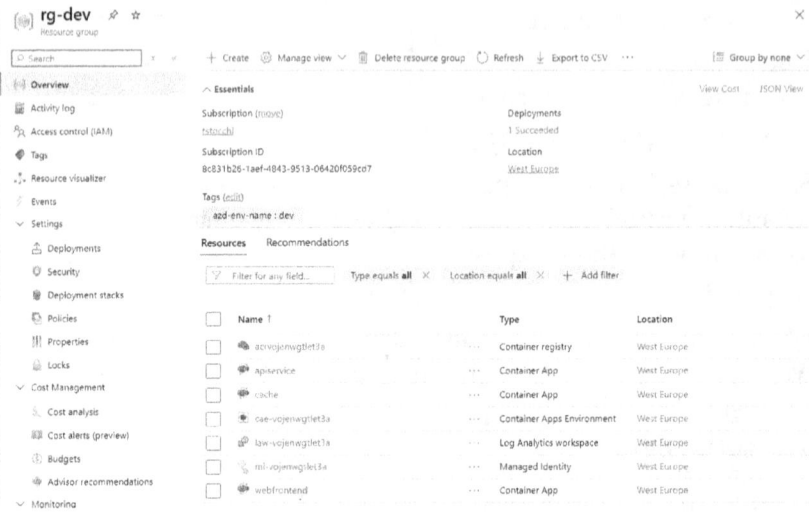

Figure 5.2: *List of resources inside the resource group inside the Azure portal*

The names of certain resources, such as the Azure Container Registry, might be different from the ones shown here because they are randomly chosen at deployment time by the Azure Developer CLI.

Now we can update our .NET Aspire template to use an Azure Redis Cache instead of a custom container.

Start by adding the required NuGet package to the AppHost project:

```
dotnet add package Aspire.Hosting.Azure.Redis
```

Change the AppHost project to use an Azure Redis Cache:

```
var builder = DistributedApplication.CreateBuilder(args);

var cache = builder.AddAzureRedis("cache");

var apiService = builder.AddProject<Projects.test_
ApiService>("apiservice");
```

First, see how the .NET Aspire manifest will reflect these changes, by re-running:

```
dotnet run --publisher manifest --output-path ../aspire-
manifest.json
```

The new manifest will provide a different description of the **cache** resource:

```
  "cache": {
    "type": "azure.bicep.v0",
  "connectionString": "{cache.outputs.connectionString}",
    "path": "cache.module.bicep",
    "params": {
      "principalId": "",
      "principalName": ""
    }
  },
```

It is now a resource of type **azure.bicep.v0** referencing the path **cache.module.bicep**. This path refers to a predefined Bicep file contained in the azd deployment files.

Now, run the **azd infra synth** command once again. The CLI will ask to overwrite the previously synthesized version. Choose to do so and see how the two **infra** folders have changed.

In the **infra** folder containing the Bicep files, there is now a **cache** folder with a **cache.module.bicep** file:

```
@description('The  location  for  the  resource(s)  to  be
deployed.')
param location string = resourceGroup().location

param principalId string

param principalName string

resource cache 'Microsoft.Cache/redis@2024-03-01' = {
  name: take('cache-${uniqueString(resourceGroup().id)}',
63)
  location: location
  properties: {
    sku: {
      name: 'Basic'
      family: 'C'
      capacity: 1
    }
    enableNonSslPort: false
```

```
    disableAccessKeyAuthentication: true
    minimumTlsVersion: '1.2'
    redisConfiguration: {
      'aad-enabled': 'true'
    }
  }
  tags: {
    'aspire-resource-name': 'cache'
  }
}

resource    cache_contributor    'Microsoft.Cache/redis/
accessPolicyAssignments@2024-03-01' = {
                                                name:
take('cachecontributor${uniqueString(resourceGroup().
id)}', 24)
  properties: {
    accessPolicyName: 'Data Contributor'
    objectId: principalId
    objectIdAlias: principalName
  }
  parent: cache
}

output  connectionString  string  =  '${cache.properties.
hostName},ssl=true'
```

This is the Bicep configuration necessary to deploy an Azure Redis Cache Resource.

Given the new nature of the Redis cache we are using, the secret containing its connection string is in the **webfrontend.tmpl.yaml** file has changed:

```
secrets:
  - name: connectionstrings--cache
    value: '{{ .Env.CACHE_CONNECTIONSTRING }}'
```

In the **infra** under the AppHost project folder, we still have the **cache.tmpl.yaml** file. This happens because the **azd infra synth** will only overwrite existing files and create new ones, but it would not delete files that are no longer needed.

This is an important point to consider: the **azd infra synth** command is useful for debugging purposes only. If you want to verify ahead of time what **azd up** will do, or if the result is not what you expected, this is a good way to understand what went wrong.

Leaving the files produced by the **azd infra synth** command in the repository, on the other hand, might lead to unexpected results. It is good practice to remove them and let the azd generate all the necessary files dynamically every time.

Development and deployment of Eshop application using azd

The first thing to consider when using the azd to deploy our Eshop application is that we are using different languages. That influenced the Aspire manifest. Launch the command to create the Aspire manifest in the **Eshop.AppHost** folder:

```
dotnet run --publisher manifest --output-path ../aspire-
manifest.json
```

The newly created **aspire-manifest.json** file looks like this:

```
{
  "$schema": "https://json.schemastore.org/aspire-
8.0.json",
  "resources": {
    "sql-password": {
      "type": "parameter.v0",
      "value": "{sql-password.inputs.value}",
      "inputs": {
        "value": {
          "type": "string"
        }
      }
    },
```

```
  "sql": {
    "type": "container.v0",
    "connectionString": "Server={sql.bindings.tcp.
host},{sql.bindings.tcp.port};User ID=sa;Password={sql-
password.value};TrustServerCertificate=true",
    "image": "mcr.microsoft.com/mssql/server:2022-
latest",
    "entrypoint": "/usr/config/entrypoint.sh",
    "bindMounts": [
      {
        "source": "Eshop.AppHost/sql-server",
        "target": "/usr/config",
        "readOnly": false
      },
      {
        "source": "../../db-scripts",
        "target": "/docker-entrypoint-initdb.d",
        "readOnly": false
      }
    ],
    "env": {
      "ACCEPT_EULA": "Y",
      "MSSQL_SA_PASSWORD": "{sql-password.value}"
    },
    "bindings": {
      "tcp": {
        "scheme": "tcp",
        "protocol": "tcp",
        "transport": "tcp",
        "targetPort": 1433
      }
    }
  },
  "WarehouseDB": {
    "type": "value.v0",
    "connectionString": "{sql.
connectionString};Database=WarehouseDB"
```

```
    },
    "dab": {
      "type": "container.v0",
      "image": "mcr.microsoft.com/azure-databases/data-
api-builder:1.2.11",
      "bindMounts": [
        {
          "source": "../../dab/dab-config.json",
          "target": "/App/dab-config.json",
          "readOnly": true
        }
      ],
      "env": {
        "ConnectionStrings__WarehouseDB": "{WarehouseDB.
connectionString}"
      },
      "bindings": {
        "http": {
          "scheme": "http",
          "protocol": "tcp",
          "transport": "http",
          "targetPort": 5000
        }
      }
    },
    "warehouseapi": {
      "type": "project.v0",
      "path": "../WarehouseAPI/WarehouseAPI.csproj",
      "env": {
        "OTEL_DOTNET_EXPERIMENTAL_OTLP_EMIT_EXCEPTION_
LOG_ATTRIBUTES": "true",
        "OTEL_DOTNET_EXPERIMENTAL_OTLP_EMIT_EVENT_LOG_
ATTRIBUTES": "true",
        "OTEL_DOTNET_EXPERIMENTAL_OTLP_RETRY": "in_
memory",
        "ASPNETCORE_FORWARDEDHEADERS_ENABLED": "true",
        "HTTP_PORTS": "{warehouseapi.bindings.http.
```

```
targetPort}",
        "services__dab__http__0": "{dab.bindings.http.
url}"
    },
    "bindings": {
      "http": {
        "scheme": "http",
        "protocol": "tcp",
        "transport": "http"
      },
      "https": {
        "scheme": "https",
        "protocol": "tcp",
        "transport": "http"
      }
    }
  },
  "create-order": {
    "type": "executable.v0",
    "workingDirectory": "../create-order-api",
    "command": "go",
    "args": [
      "run",
      "."
    ],
    "env": {
      "PORT": "{create-order.bindings.http.
targetPort}",
      "services__dab__http__0": "{dab.bindings.http.
url}"
    },
    "bindings": {
      "http": {
        "scheme": "http",
        "protocol": "tcp",
        "transport": "http",
        "port": 5001,
```

```
          "targetPort": 8000
        }
      }
    },
    "process-payment": {
      "type": "executable.v0",
      "workingDirectory": "../process-payment-api",
      "command": "uv",
      "args": [
        "run",
        "process-payment-api"
      ],
      "env": {
        "PORT": "{process-payment.bindings.http.
targetPort}",
        "services__dab__http__0": "{dab.bindings.http.
url}"
      },
      "bindings": {
        "http": {
          "scheme": "http",
          "protocol": "tcp",
          "transport": "http",
          "port": 5002,
          "targetPort": 8001
        }
      }
    },
    "ship-api": {
      "type": "executable.v0",
      "workingDirectory": "../shipping-api/src",
      "command": "node",
      "args": [
        "index.js"
      ],
      "env": {
        "NODE_ENV": "development",
```

```
      "PORT": "{ship-api.bindings.http.targetPort}",
      "services__dab__http__0": "{dab.bindings.http.
url}"
    },
    "bindings": {
      "http": {
        "scheme": "http",
        "protocol": "tcp",
        "transport": "http",
        "port": 5003,
        "targetPort": 8002
      }
    }
  },
  "FrontendWithReact": {
    "type": "dockerfile.v0",
    "path": "../FrontendWithReact/frontend-react-app/
Dockerfile",
    "context": "../FrontendWithReact/frontend-react-
app",
    "env": {
      "NODE_ENV": "development",
      "services__warehouseapi__http__0":
"{warehouseapi.bindings.http.url}",
      "services__warehouseapi__https__0":
"{warehouseapi.bindings.https.url}",
      "services__create-order__http__0": "{create-
order.bindings.http.url}",
      "services__process-payment__http__0": "{process-
payment.bindings.http.url}",
      "services__ship-api__http__0": "{ship-api.
bindings.http.url}",
      "PORT": "{FrontendWithReact.bindings.http.
targetPort}",
      "BROWSER": "none"
    },
    "bindings": {
      "http": {
```

```
        "scheme": "http",
        "protocol": "tcp",
        "transport": "http",
        "targetPort": 8003,
        "external": true
      }
    }
  }
 }
}
```

The **create-order, process-payment,** and **ship-api** are of type **executable.v0**. The frontend is of type **dockerfile.v0**. That is because we have specified **.PublishAsDockerfile()** for the frontend, but not for the other APIs.

This will cause **azd up** to fail, because it has no knowledge of how to transform an unspecified executable resource into a container. For .NET projects, it is easy because azd is instructed to run the command to have .NET generate the Dockerfile, as shown in the previous example.

.PusblishAsDockerfile() will automatically search for a Dockerfile in the root folder of the selected resource. It can also be configured to search the Dockerfile in other paths.

Therefore, we need to add the **.PublishAsDockerfile()** in each of those resources and create a Dockerfile in the root folder of each of those microservices.

Start by updating the configuration of the executable resources:

```
var createOrderApi = builder.AddGolangApp("create-order",
"../../create-order-api")
    .WithHttpEndpoint(env: "PORT")
    .WithReference(dab)
    .WaitFor(dab)
    .PublishAsDockerFile();

var processPaymentApi = builder.AddUvApp("process-
payment", "../../process-payment-api", "process-payment-
api")
```

```
    .WithHttpEndpoint(env: "PORT")
    .WithReference(dab)
    .WaitFor(dab)
    .PublishAsDockerFile();
```

```
var shippingApi = builder.AddNodeApp("ship-api", "src/
index.js", "../../shipping-api")
    .WithNpmPackageInstallation()
    .WithHttpEndpoint(env: "PORT")
    .WithReference(dab)
    .WaitFor(dab)
    .PublishAsDockerFile();
```

Now, only when the AppHost project is running in deployment mode (**dotnet run --publisher manifest**), it will describe those resources as **dockerfile.v0**. When running it locally, they will start as an executable.

Create a file named Dockerfile under the **create-order-api** folder:

```
# Use the official Golang image as the base image
FROM golang:1.23

# Set the working directory inside the container
WORKDIR /app

# Copy go.mod and go.sum files
COPY go.mod go.sum ./

# Download dependencies
RUN go mod download

# Copy the source code into the container
COPY . .

# Build the application
RUN go build -o main .

# Expose port 8000
```

```
EXPOSE 8000

# Command to run the application
CMD ["./main"]
```

Create a file named Dockerfile under the **process-payment-api** folder:

```
# Use the official Python image as the base image
FROM python:3.13-slim-bookworm
COPY --from=ghcr.io/astral-sh/uv:latest /uv /uvx /bin/

# Copy the project into the image
ADD . /app

# Sync the project into a new environment, using the
frozen lockfile
WORKDIR /app
RUN uv sync --frozen

# Expose the port the application will run on
EXPOSE 8001

# Command to run the application
CMD ["uv", "run", "process-payment-api"]
```

Make sure to also create a **.dockerignore** and add the **.venv** folder in it:

.venv/

__pycache__/

Create a file named Dockerfile under the **shipping-api** folder:

```
# Use the official Node.js image as the base image
FROM node:20

# Set the working directory inside the container
WORKDIR /app

# Copy package.json and package-lock.json to the working
```

```
directory
COPY package.json package-lock.json ./

# Install dependencies
RUN npm install

# Copy the rest of the application code to the working
directory
COPY . .

# Expose the port the app runs on
EXPOSE 8000

# Define the command to run the application
CMD ["npm", "start"]
```

Now you can run:

azd config set alpha.azd.operations on

azd init

azd up

Once the deployment is completed, you will see a success message at the end in the terminal as shown in *Figure 5.3*:

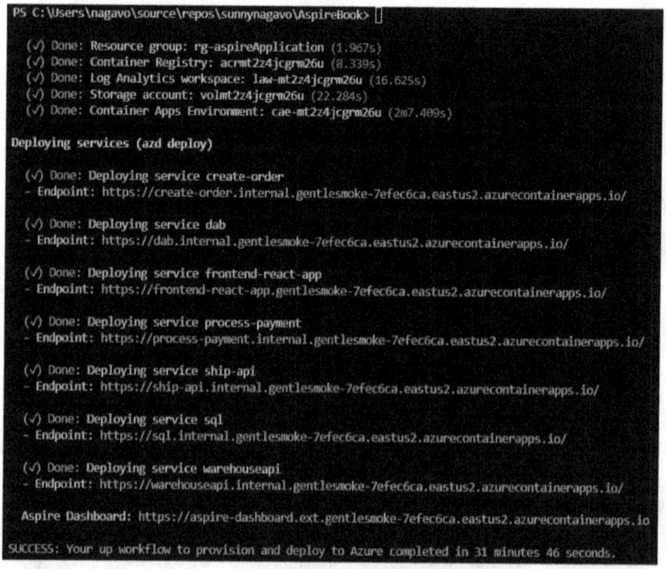

Figure 5.3: Successfully deployed all the resources using azd up command

We are setting the **alpha.azd.operations** flag to **on** because it enables the azd to upload the bind-mounted files.

You can call the environment however you see fit. We have opted to call it **eshop-aspire**.

Open the SQL Container App, go to the **Containers** section, and move to the **Environment variables** tab to set the **MSSQL_SA_PASSWORD** variable as shown in *Figure 5.4*:

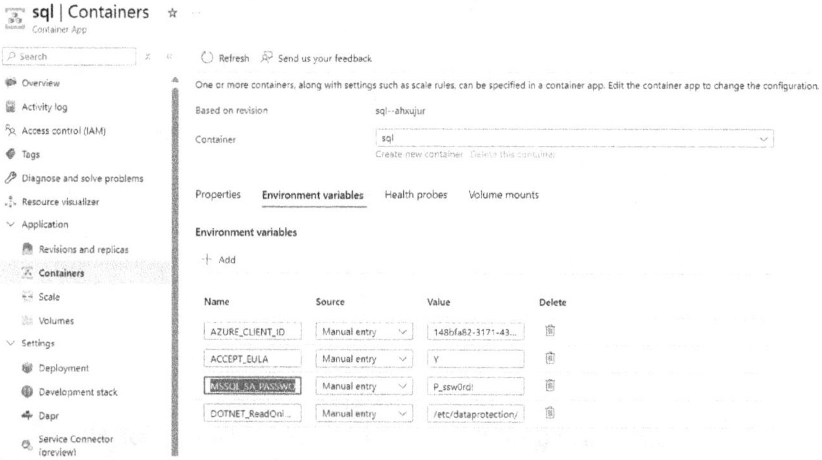

Figure 5.4: Shows a list of environment variables for SQL container

You also need to update the entry point for the container with the script we use locally for Docker, as shown in *Figure 5.5*:

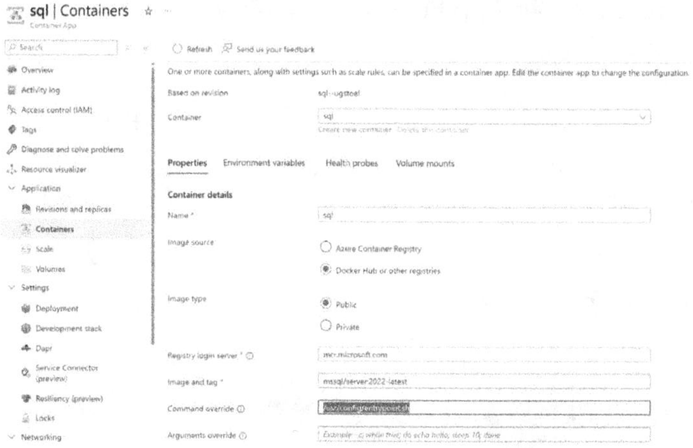

Figure 5.5: Shows the properties view to update command override with entry point script

Once the modified changes to the container properties are saved, it will automatically deploy as a new version.

Once the SQL container has been updated, we can update the **dab** resource as well to add the **dab-config.json** parameter in the **Sub path** section as shown in *Figure 5.6*:

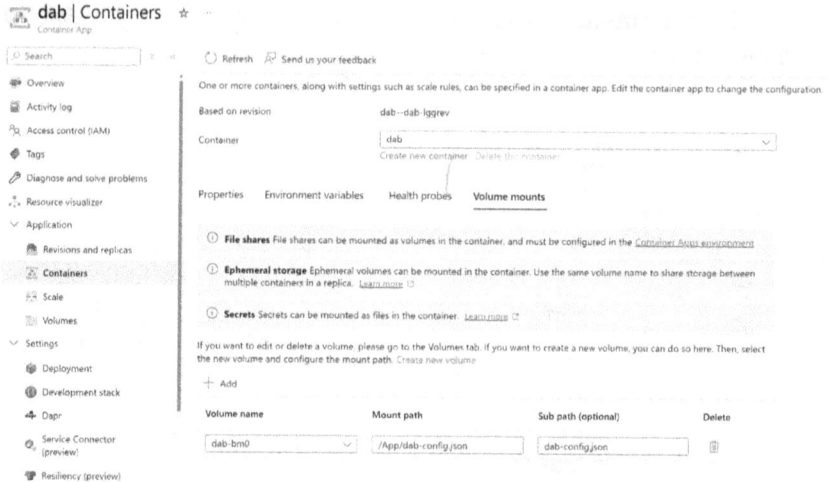

Figure 5.6: Updating sub path section to reference dab-config.json file

Like SQL container, once modified, save changes to the dab container to deploy as a new revision.

You should be able to navigate to the Aspire dashboard deployed in the Azure Container App Environment as shown in *Figure 5.7*:

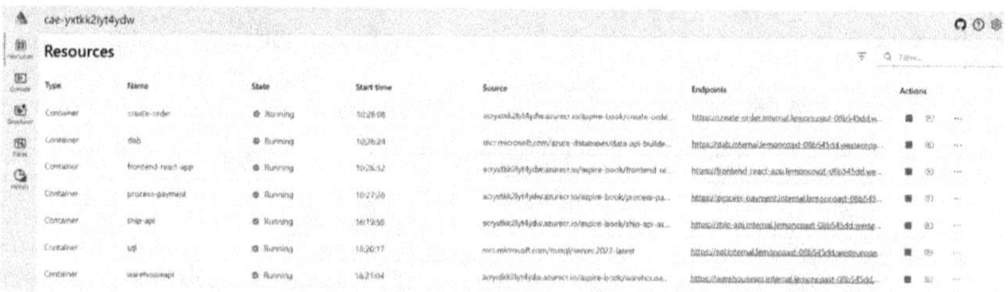

Figure 5.7: .NET Aspire dashboard with complete list of resources in healthy state

Advanced azd features

The azd can help you configure a CI/CD pipeline for both GitHub and Azure DevOps.

To start, launch this command in an already initialized azd repository:

azd pipeline config

The CLI will ask to choose between GitHub and Azure DevOps. Choose GitHub to follow this sample.

It will scan the repository and ask you for permission to create the basic **azure-dev.yml** workflow file. Accept the proceed to the next step, in which the CLI will create a service principal on Azure and set all the required secrets in the GitHub repository secrets section.

Lastly, it will ask for permission to commit and push all the local changes to trigger the newly created pipeline on GitHub.

The pipeline that has been created for us looks like this:

```
# Run when commits are pushed to main
on:
  workflow_dispatch:
  push:
    # Run when commits are pushed to mainline branch
(main or master)
    # Set this to the mainline branch you are using
    branches:
      - main


# Set up permissions for deploying with secretless Azure
federated credentials
# https://learn.microsoft.com/en-us/azure/developer/
github/connect-from-azure?tabs=azure-portal%2Clinux#set-
up-azure-login-with-openid-connect-authentication
permissions:
  id-token: write
  contents: read


jobs:
  build:
    runs-on: ubuntu-latest
    env:
      AZURE_CLIENT_ID: ${{ vars.AZURE_CLIENT_ID }}
```

```
        AZURE_TENANT_ID: ${{ vars.AZURE_TENANT_ID }}
        AZURE_SUBSCRIPTION_ID: ${{ vars.AZURE_SUBSCRIPTION_
ID }}
        AZURE_ENV_NAME: ${{ vars.AZURE_ENV_NAME }}
        AZURE_LOCATION: ${{ vars.AZURE_LOCATION }}
    steps:
      - name: Checkout
        uses: actions/checkout@v4
      - name: Install azd
        uses: Azure/setup-azd@v2
      - name: Setup .NET
        uses: actions/setup-dotnet@v4
        with:
          dotnet-version: |
            8.x.x
            9.x.x

      - name: Log in with Azure (Federated Credentials)
        run: |
          azd auth login `
            --client-id "$Env:AZURE_CLIENT_ID" `
            --federated-credential-provider "github" `
            --tenant-id "$Env:AZURE_TENANT_ID"
        shell: pwsh


      - name: Provision Infrastructure
        run: azd provision --no-prompt
        env:
          AZD_INITIAL_ENVIRONMENT_CONFIG: ${{ secrets.
AZD_INITIAL_ENVIRONMENT_CONFIG }}

      - name: Deploy Application
        run: azd deploy --no-prompt
```

The workflow is a multi-step CI/CD pipeline that will install azd and .NET on the agent, log in with Azure, and use the two basic commands of the azd to provision the infrastructure and deploy the code.

Conclusion

In this chapter, we explored the azd, a developer-friendly tool for streamlining the deployment of distributed applications, especially those built with .NET Aspire. We learned that azd simplifies the deployment process by using templates, scanning codebases, and provisioning infrastructure with Bicep files. We covered azd's installation, configuration, and its use with both sample templates and .NET Aspire applications. Using the azd up command, developers can provision and deploy their applications efficiently in a single step.

We also discussed the dynamic generation of Bicep files by azd, based on the .NET Aspire manifest, which describes the application's architecture and resources. We explored deploying applications to Azure with azd up, managing environment variables, and transitioning between different types of resources. The chapter concluded by applying these concepts to a more complex multi-language, multi-service application and setting up a CI/CD pipeline using azd, highlighting its effectiveness in automating the deployment process.

In the next chapter, we will introduce **Distributed Application Runtime (Dapr)** along with its architecture and its role in building resilient, microservice-based applications. We will also explore how to deploy Dapr-integrated .NET Aspire applications to Azure.

Join our Discord space

Join our Discord workspace for latest updates, offers, tech happenings around the world, new releases, and sessions with the authors:

https://discord.bpbonline.com

CHAPTER 6
Integrating with Dapr

Introduction

When .NET Aspire was released, many developers began asking if there was an overlap with another popular open-source tool called Dapr. Dapr also aims to make life easier when working with distributed applications. While both aim to ease the complexities of microservices, they serve different purposes and can complement each other. In this chapter, we will have an overview of what Dapr is, why it does not really overlap with .NET Aspire, and how it can work with .NET Aspire.

Structure

In this chapter, we will discuss the following topics:

- Distributed Application Runtime
- Importance of Dapr
- Getting started with Dapr

- Using Dapr in .NET Aspire
- Configuring Dapr for Azure deployment

Objectives

By the end of the chapter, you will learn about Dapr architecture and its role in building resilient, microservice-based applications. You will understand the differences between Dapr and .NET Aspire, clarifying their distinct purposes and how you can use Dapr to further improve your developer experience when working with .NET Aspire in building reliable distributed applications. Finally, this chapter aims to provide you with a detailed understanding of considerations for deploying Dapr-integrated .NET Aspire applications to Azure.

Distributed Application Runtime

Dapr is a portable, event-driven runtime that makes it easy for developers to build resilient, microservices-based applications. Dapr provides a set of building blocks that developers can use to build their applications, including state management, publisher/subscriber messaging - in short we call it as **publisher/subscriber (pub/sub)** messaging, and service invocation. A building block is nothing but an HTTP or gRPC API that can be called from your application code and uses one or more Dapr components. These building blocks are designed to be language-agnostic, so developers can use them with any programming language. *Figure 6.1* shows the list of various building blocks that Dapr provides. In this chapter, we will mainly look into the Service Invocation and Publish/Subscribe building blocks.

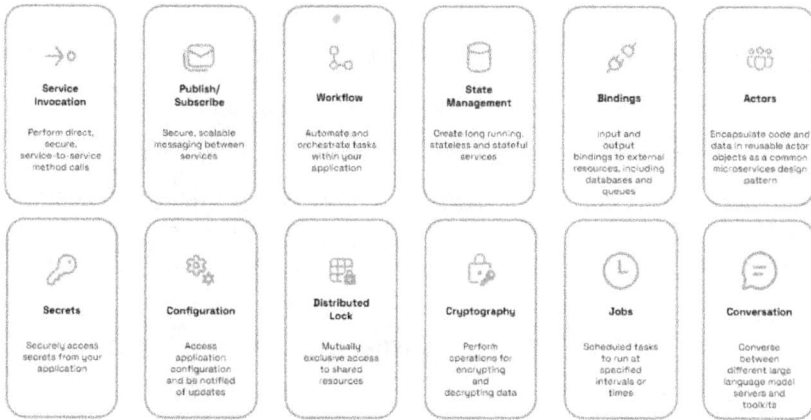

Figure 6.1: Dapr building blocks

Dapr uses the sidecar architecture pattern. Basically, our microservice does not talk to the Redis cache or the **application programming interface** (**API**) service directly. Instead, it talks to the Dapr sidecar, which, in turn, talks to the cache or the API service. This allows Dapr to provide a consistent interface for all the building blocks, regardless of the underlying implementation. The underlying technology can be easily switched using different configuration files written in YAML.

Dapr's ability to perform service-to-service invocations can be thought of as the only common ground this runtime has with .NET Aspire. If we have two generic services, called ServiceA and ServiceB, using Dapr, we can invoke ServiceB from ServiceA, performing an HTTP call to ServiceA's Dapr sidecar. This sidecar then handles the communication and forwards the request to ServiceB's Dapr sidecar, which ultimately reaches ServiceB.

The HTTP endpoint URL Dapr uses for service to service invocation is shown in the following. Let us try to break it down:

```
"http://localhost:<DAPR_SIDECAR_PORT>/v1.0/
invoke/<ServiceB>/method/<PATH_TO_INVOKE>"
```

- **DAPR_SIDECAR_PORT**: This needs to be replaced with the actual port number of Dapr Sidecar running alongside the calling service.

- **/v1.0/invoke/**: This is the Dapr API endpoint for invoking another service.

- **<ServiceB>**: This is the App ID of the target service to be invoked. Dapr uses App IDs to identify services.

- **/method/<PATH_TO_INVOKE>**: This specifies the specific method or endpoint on ServiceB that you want to execute.

For example, let us say, we have a Dapr sidecar for ServiceA running on port 3500. The Appid of ServiceB is **my-service-b**, and you would like to invoke the **get-info** method on ServiceB. Then the actual URL would become:

```
http://localhost:3500/v1.0/invoke/my-service-b/method/
get-info
```

It is the developer's choice whether to rely on the service discovery offered by .NET Aspire or the service-to-service invocation provided by Dapr. Nonetheless, it is worth noting that using service-to-service invocation will result in more HTTP invocations. ServiceA will invoke its sidecar, ServiceA's sidecar will invoke the name resolution component to identify which service ServiceB is and proceed to forward the request to ServiceB's sidecar, and ServiceB's sidecar will invoke ServiceB. The inverse path will be taken to return an answer from ServiceB to ServiceA, as shown in the following figure:

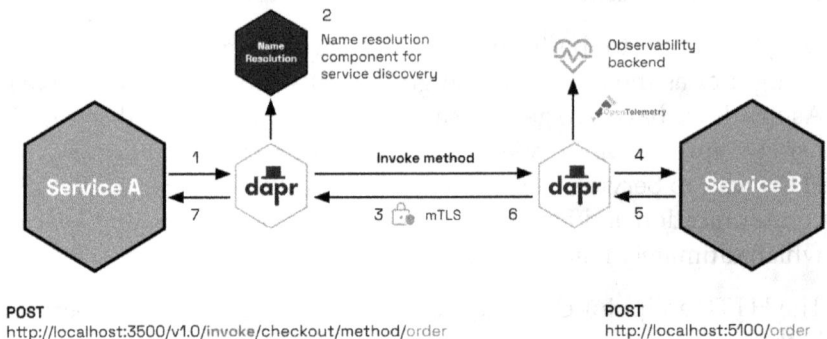

Figure 6.2: Dapr service-to-service invocation

Importance of Dapr

In our e-commerce application, we are going to use Dapr to handle the configuration of the publish/subscribe component. This is a great pattern to improve distributed applications' scalability and resiliency. Instead of having ServiceA talk with ServiceB, ServiceA will publish a message in a subscription topic. ServiceB will subscribe to that topic, and whenever a new message is in the queue, it will be able to read the message and perform some actions. This way, if ServiceB is busy handling previous requests, ServiceA will not have to wait for ServiceB to be available. ServiceA will publish its message in the topic, and ServiceB will handle the message when ready.

There are many cloud and on-premise resources that can be used to implement a publish/subscribe pattern: Redis Streams, RabbitMQTT, Azure Service Bus Topics, **Amazon Web Services (AWS) Simple Notification Service/Simple Queue Service (SNS/SQS)**, and **Google Cloud Platform (GCP)** and pub/sub are amongst the common ones.

Using Dapr, we can use a generic interface for a pub/sub resource and simply switch between them by changing the configuration YAML file.

Dapr offers native SDKs for many coding languages. If the SDK is not available for a certain language, the Dapr sidecar can be invoked via HTTP request. Therefore, it can be used with any coding language as long as it offers an HTTP client.

Getting started with Dapr

To integrate Dapr with .NET Aspire, you will first need to set up Dapr on your local development machine. This involves installing and initializing the Dapr **command line interface (CLI)** locally. The official documentation is quite clear (refer to **https://docs.dapr. io/getting-started/install-dapr-cli/**), and you can follow the steps needed based on your machine's operating system:

1. **Install Dapr CLI on Windows machine**: Install the latest Windows Dapr CLI to **$Env:SystemDrive\dapr** and add this directory to the user PATH environment variable:

    ```
    powershell -Command "iwr -useb https://raw.
    githubusercontent.com/dapr/cli/master/install/
    install.ps1 | iex"
    ```

2. **Install using winget**: Install the latest Windows Dapr CLI to **$Env:SystemDrive\dapr** and add this directory to the user PATH environment variable by running the following command:

    ```
    winget install Dapr.CLI
    ```

At the time of writing this book, Dapr had released the 1.15.0 version, which was installed on my machine as shown in *Figure 6.3*:

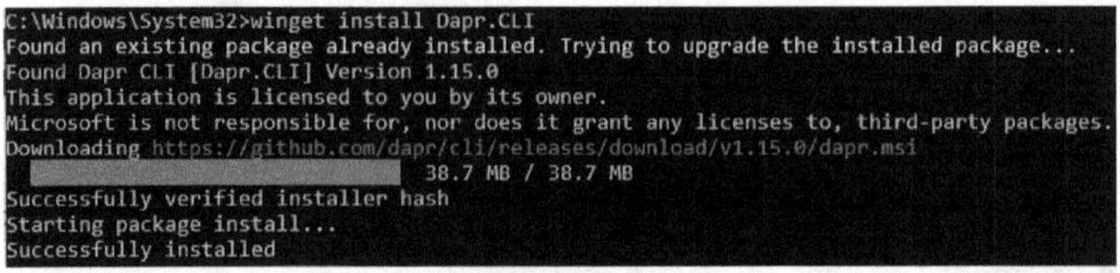

```
C:\Windows\System32>winget install Dapr.CLI
Found an existing package already installed. Trying to upgrade the installed package...
Found Dapr CLI [Dapr.CLI] Version 1.15.0
This application is licensed to you by its owner.
Microsoft is not responsible for, nor does it grant any licenses to, third-party packages.
Downloading https://github.com/dapr/cli/releases/download/v1.15.0/dapr.msi
                                  38.7 MB / 38.7 MB
Successfully verified installer hash
Starting package install...
Successfully installed
```

Figure 6.3: Dapr installation via winget

Verify the CLI is installed by restarting your terminal/command prompt and running the following command, which will show output as shown in *Figure 6.3*:

```
dapr -h
```

The expected output is shown in the following figure after running the above command:

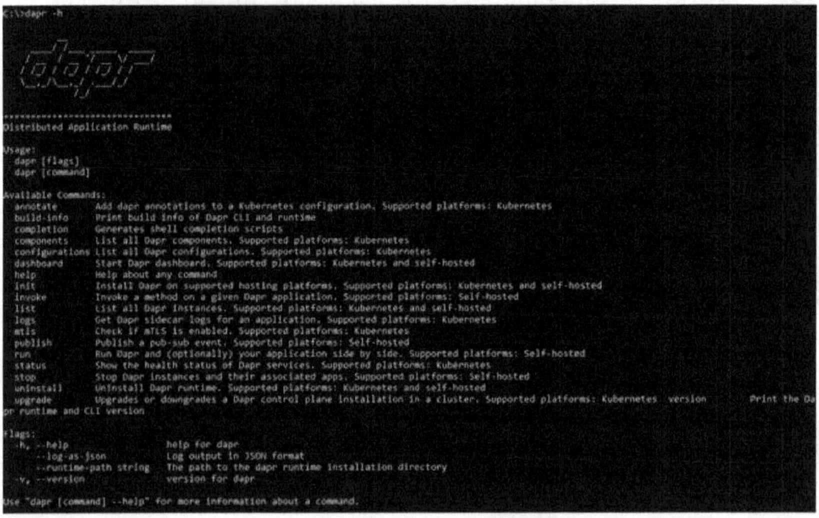

Figure 6.4: Dapr help command output, which shows list of available commands

Now that you have verified the installation of Dapr CLI, use the CLI to initialize Dapr runtime binaries on your local machine by running the following command:

```
dapr init
```

The expected output is shown in the following figure after running above command:

```
C:\Windows\System32>dapr init
Making the jump to hyperspace...
Container images will be pulled from Docker Hub
Installing runtime version 1.14.4
Downloading binaries and setting up components...
Downloaded binaries and completed components set up.
daprd binary has been installed to C:\Users\nagavo\.dapr\bin.
dapr_placement container is running.
dapr_redis container is running.
dapr_zipkin container is running.
dapr_scheduler container is running.
Use `docker ps` to check running containers.
Success! Dapr is up and running. To get started, go here: https://docs.dapr.io/getting-started
```

Figure 6.5: Running Dapr init command

Verify the Dapr version by running the following command:

dapr --version

This displays the installed CLI and runtime versions, as shown in the following figure:

```
C:\Windows\System32>dapr --version
CLI version: 1.15.0
Runtime version: 1.14.4
```

Figure 6.6: Displays installed Dapr version

Using Dapr in .NET Aspire

Similar to using different languages and adding databases and containers, Dapr can be used with .NET Aspire as an integration. This integration is managed in the CommunityToolkit repository.

We will begin by adding the hosting integration for Dapr to our AppHost project. In the Eshop.AppHost project, we first need to add the correct NuGet package:

dotnet add package CommunityToolkit.Aspire.Hosting.Dapr

To add a pub/sub Dapr component, we can add this line of code in the **Program.cs** of the **Eshop.AppHost** project:

var pubsub = builder.AddDaprPubSub("pubsub");

This way, .NET Aspire will use the default Dapr pub/sub component. The definition of this default component is stored in the **C:\ Users\<USERNAME>\.dapr\components** folder:

```
apiVersion: dapr.io/v1alpha1
kind: Component
```

```
metadata:
  name: pubsub
spec:
  type: pubsub.redis
  version: v1
  metadata:
  - name: redisHost
    value: localhost:6379
  - name: redisPassword
    value: ""
```

As we can see, it uses Redis. If we have correctly initialized Dapr on our machine, we should have a **dapr_redis** container running. This container is a Redis instance used by Dapr for both the default pub/sub component and statestore component.

Now that we have added a Dapr pub/sub component to the AppHost, we can start using it in our APIs.

The warehouse API does not need to subscribe to a topic because it handles a simple request that needs to return information to the frontend. The pipeline to process an order is a good scenario where the publisher/subscriber pattern can improve performance. The frontend will invoke the create order via HTTP. Create an order and publish a message to process the payment. Once the payment has been processed, the Process Payment API will publish a message to handle the order shipment.

We will begin by updating the create order API to use Dapr.

First, we need to reference the newly created pub/sub component in the **createOrderApi** resource:

```
var createOrderApi = builder.AddGolangApp("create-order",
"../../create-order-api")
    .WithHttpEndpoint(port: 5001, env: "PORT")
    .WithReference(dab)
    .WaitFor(dab)
    .WithDaprSidecar(new DaprSidecarOptions(){ AppPort =
5001, AppId = "create-order" })
    .WithReference(pubsub);
```

The **WithDaprSidecar** method ensures that this resource will have a Dapr Sidecar, and the **WithReference(pubsub)** will make the pub/sub component available to this resource.

To use Dapr in Golang, first, we need to add the required modules:

```
go get "github.com/dapr/go-sdk/client"
go install "github.com/dapr/go-sdk/client"
```

The following the official Dapr documentation, we need to use the Dapr Client to publish the message after the order has been created:

- **First, update the imports**:

```
import (
    "context"
    "encoding/json"
    "io/ioutil"
    "log"
    "main/otelx"
    "net/http"
    "os"
    "strconv"
    "strings"
    "time"

    dapr "github.com/dapr/go-sdk/client"
    "github.com/gin-gonic/gin"
    "go.opentelemetry.io/contrib/instrumentation/
github.com/gin-gonic/gin/otelgin"
    "go.opentelemetry.io/otel"
    "go.opentelemetry.io/otel/metric"
)
```

- **Add this code at the end of the POST request handling method**:

```
daprClient, err := dapr.NewClient()
        if err != nil {
            panic(err)
        }
        defer daprClient.Close()
```

```go
//Using Dapr SDK to publish a topic
body, err := ioutil.ReadAll(resp.Body)
if err != nil {
    return
}

var response struct {
    Value []struct {
        OrderID int `json:"OrderID"`
    } `json:"value"`
}

if err := json.Unmarshal(body, &response);
err != nil {
    return
}

if len(response.Value) == 0 {
    return
}

orderID := strconv.Itoa(response.Value[0].
OrderID)
log.Printf("Order ID: %s", orderID)
ctx := context.Background()
if err := daprClient.PublishEvent(ctx,
"pubsub", "process-payment", []byte(orderID)); err
!= nil {
    panic(err)
}
```

Adding Dapr to the remaining APIs

Now that the Create Order API uses the Dapr pub/sub component, we can focus on the Process Payment API.

Process Payment API is written using FastAPI, a framework that natively supports Dapr. Therefore, we do not need to change the structure of the web server, but we still have to make a few updates.

Start by adding the Dapr sidecar and reference to the pub/sub resource to the **processPaymentAPI**:

```
var processPaymentApi = builder.AddUvApp("process-
payment", "../../process-payment-api", "process-payment-
api")
    .WithHttpEndpoint(port: 5002, env: "PORT")
    .WithReference(dab)
    .WaitFor(dab)
    .WithDaprSidecar(new DaprSidecarOptions(){ AppPort =
5002, AppId = "process-payment" })
    .WithReference(pubusb);
```

Open a terminal in the **process-payment-api** folder and run the command to add the DaprFastAPI extension using the **uv** package manager:

uv pip install dapr

uv pip install dapr-ext-fastapi

Then, update the code according to the official Dapr documentation for FastAPI:

```
from fastapi import Body, FastAPI, HTTPException
from dapr.clients import DaprClient
from dapr.ext.fastapi import DaprApp
from pydantic import BaseModel
import uvicorn
import os
import requests
import json
from datetime import datetime

app = FastAPI()
dapr_app = DaprApp(app)

class PaymentPayload(BaseModel):
```

```
    OrderID: str

@dapr_app.subscribe(pubsub='pubsub', topic='process-
payment')
@app.post("/api/process-payment")
def process_payment(event_data = Body()):
    data = event_data.get("data")
    order_id = data.get("OrderID")
    if not order_id:
        raise HTTPException(status_code=400,
detail="Payload must contain 'OrderID'")

    api_endpoint = os.environ.get("services__dab__
http__0")
    if not api_endpoint:
        raise HTTPException(status_code=500,
detail="Environment variable 'services__dab__http__0' is
not set")

    # Read the order with OrderID from the same endpoint
    url = f"{api_endpoint}/api/Orders/OrderID/{order_id}"
    response = requests.get(url)
    if response.status_code != 200:
        raise HTTPException(status_code=500,
detail=f"Failed to retrieve order: {response.text}")

    order_data = response.json()

    # Extract the first item from the array
    order_data = order_data["value"][0]

    # Remove the OrderID field from the order data
    if "OrderID" in order_data:
        del order_data["OrderID"]
    # Update the order data
    order_data["Status"] = "processing"
    order_data["LastUpdated"] = datetime.utcnow().
```

```
isoformat()

    # Print the updated order data for debug purposes
    print("Updated order data:", order_data)

    # Send the updated order data as an update request
    response = requests.put(url, json=order_data)
    if response.status_code != 200:
        raise HTTPException(status_code=500,
detail=f"Failed to update order status: {response.text}")

    PUBSUB_NAME = 'pubsub'
    TOPIC_NAME = 'ship-order'
    with DaprClient() as client:
        #Using Dapr SDK to publish a topic
        result = client.publish_event(
            pubsub_name=PUBSUB_NAME,
            topic_name=TOPIC_NAME,
            data=json.dumps({"OrderID": order_id}),
            data_content_type='application/json',
        )

    return response.json()

def main() -> None:
    port = int(os.environ.get("PORT", 8000))
    uvicorn.run(app, host="127.0.0.1", port=port)
```

We need to import the class Body from FastAPI and change the received payload type to Body because the endpoint is now receiving custom events from the pub/sub topic. We also need to add the line to define to which topic of which Dapr pub/sub component our method needs to subscribe to:

@dapr_app.subscribe(pubsub='pubsub',topic='process-payment')

The final part of the API uses a DaprClient to publish a new message on the **ship-order** topic.

To test our new service, open a command line and start a headless Dapr application:

```
dapr run --app-id ordersubmitter --dapr-http-port 3601
```

This application will be able to publish a message on the queue. To publish a message, we can simply use Dapr APIs. In Visual Studio Code, create a new **test.http** file and add this:

```
POST    http://localhost:3601/v1.0/publish/pubsub/process-payment
Content-Type: application/json


{
    "OrderID": "1"
}
```

You should see via Data API Builder that the order with ID **1** is now in the **processing** state.

The last API we need to update is **shippingApi**, which is written in NodeJS:

```
var shippingApi = builder.AddNodeApp("ship-api", "index.js", "../../shipping-api/src")
    .WithNpmPackageInstallation()
    .WithHttpEndpoint(port: 5003, env: "PORT")
    .WithReference(dab)
    .WaitFor(dab)
    .WithDaprSidecar(new DaprSidecarOptions(){ AppPort = 5003, AppId = "shipping-api" })
    .WithReference(pubusb);
```

According to the official Dapr documentation, we can use the **DaprServer** with our own express webserver:

```
const { DaprServer, CommunicationProtocolEnum } = require("@dapr/dapr");
const express = require('express');
const axios = require('axios');
const bodyParser = require('body-parser');

const app = express();
```

```
app.use(bodyParser.json());

app.post('/api/ship-product', async (req, res) => {
    const { OrderID } = req.body;
    if (!OrderID) {
        return res.status(400).json({ detail: "Payload
must contain 'OrderID'" });
    }

    try {
        await UpdateOrderStatus(OrderID);

        res.json(response.data);
    } catch (error) {
        res.status(500).json({ detail: `Error processing
request: ${error.message}` });
    }
});

(async () => {
    const daprServer = new DaprServer({
        serverHost: "127.0.0.1",
        serverPort: process.env.PORT || 8000,
        serverHttp: app,
        clientOptions: {
            daprPort: process.env.DAPR_HTTP_PORT || 3500,
        },
    });

    await daprServer.pubsub.subscribe("pubsub", "ship-
order", async (data) => {
        const OrderID = data.OrderID;
        console.log("Received event data:", JSON.
stringify(OrderID, null, 2));
        await UpdateOrderStatus(OrderID);
        console.log(`Order ${OrderID} status updated.`);
    });
```

```javascript
    await daprServer.start();
  })().catch(console.error);

async function UpdateOrderStatus(orderID) {
    const apiEndpoint = process.env.services__dab__
http__0;

    // Read the order with OrderID from the same endpoint
    const url = `${apiEndpoint}/api/Orders/
OrderID/${orderID}`;
    let response = await axios.get(url);
    if (response.status !== 200) {
        throw new Error(`Failed to retrieve order:
${response.data}`);
    }

    let orderData = response.data.value[0];

    // Remove the OrderID field from the order data
    delete orderData.OrderID;

    // Update the order data
    orderData.Status = "completed";
    orderData.LastUpdated = new Date().toISOString();

    // Print the updated order data for debug purposes
    console.log("Updated order data:", JSON.
stringify(orderData, null, 2));

    // Update the order data
    const config = {
        headers: {
            'Content-Type': 'application/json'
        }
    };
    response = await axios.put(url, JSON.
```

```
stringify(orderData, null, 2), config);

    // Update the warehouse stock based on the order
details
    const warehouseUrl = `${apiEndpoint}/api/
WarehouseItems/ItemID/${orderData.ItemID}`;
    let warehouseResponse = await axios.
get(warehouseUrl);
    let warehouseItem = warehouseResponse.data.value[0];
    warehouseItem.Stock -= orderData.Quantity;
    delete warehouseItem.ItemID;

    // Print the updated warehouse quantity for debug
purposes
    console.log("Updated warehouse data:", JSON.
stringify(warehouseItem, null, 2));

    await axios.put(warehouseUrl, JSON.
stringify(warehouseItem, null, 2), config);
}
```

We also need to update the dependencies in the **package.json**:

```
"dependencies": {
    "axios": "^0.21.1",
    "body-parser": "^1.19.0",
    "express": "^4.17.1",
    "@dapr/dapr": "^3.5.2"
  }
```

Configuring Dapr for Azure deployment

The Dapr integration for .NET Aspire is currently being rethought from the ground up. The basic concepts we have shown in this chapter would not change. The logic with which you can configure your custom Dapr components and handle the deployment of the configured resources is different.

In the Community Toolkit for .NET Aspire repo, there are three NuGet packages about Dapr:

- **CommunityToolkit.Aspire.Hosting.Dapr** is the one we have been using so far
- **CommunityToolkit.Aspire.Hosting.Azure.Dapr**
- **CommunityToolkit.Aspire.Hosting.Azure.Dapr.Redis**

The two new NuGet packages allow the developer to write the following set of instructions in the AppHost:

```
var builder = DistributedApplication.CreateBuilder(args);

var redisState = builder.AddAzureRedis("redisState")
                        .RunAsContainer(); // for local
development

var daprState = builder.AddDaprStateStore("daprState")
                        .WithReference(redisState); //
instructs aspire to use azure redis when publishing

var api = builder.AddProject<Projects.
MyApiService>("example-api")
    .WithReference(daprState)
    .WithDaprSidecar();

builder.Build().Run();
```

Doing so, we are capable of defining our own instance of an Azure Redis Cache, which will run locally as a normal Redis container, and will be used by Dapr as a statestore component.

There is still a way to configure a custom Dapr component using YAML files, and that can be achieved by using the generic **AddDaprComponent** method:

```
builder.AddDaprComponent("custompubsub", "pubsub", new
DaprComponentOptions(){
    LocalPath = "pubsub.yaml",
});
```

Conclusion

In this chapter, we explored integrating Dapr with .NET Aspire, clarifying differences between them in building distributed applications. We examined Dapr's sidecar architecture and building blocks like service invocation and publish/subscribe, highlighting its language-agnostic nature and pluggable components, which complements .NET Aspire's orchestration and service discovery.

We provided practical guidance on setting up Dapr locally, integrating it into .NET Aspire applications, and using it with various APIs (Golang, FastAPI, Node.js). We demonstrated how Dapr enhances scalability and resiliency through patterns like publish/subscribe. We touched upon configuring Dapr for Azure deployment, including integration within the Community Toolkit for .NET Aspire, newer NuGet packages for streamlined component deployment, and using YAML files for custom configuration. This chapter equips developers to leverage Dapr's benefits in their .NET Aspire applications.

In the next chapter, we will discuss unit testing our application.

Join our Discord space

Join our Discord workspace for latest updates, offers, tech happenings around the world, new releases, and sessions with the authors:

https://discord.bpbonline.com

CHAPTER 7

.NET Aspire Testing

Introduction

Microservices emerged as a powerful architecture in building scalable, resilient, and maintainable applications. With the increasing popularity of microservices, software development demands the need for different strategies for testing distributed applications. Unit testing is particularly important because each service plays a critical role in the functionality of the overall application. A failure in the warehouse API could lead to incorrect inventory information, which could result in orders not being fulfilled correctly. In this chapter, we will discuss unit testing in the context of our Eshop application by introducing unit tests for one of our API services and discussing the importance of Integration testing. Without unit testing, issues could surface in production that could have been caught early during integration.

Structure

In this chapter, we will discuss the following topics:

- Importance of testing in distributed systems
- Testing in .NET Aspire
- Setting up test projects in .NET Aspire
- Introduction to unit testing

Objectives

By the end of the chapter, you will learn about the role of unit testing in microservices, how to set up different testing projects within the .NET Aspire solution, and how to write, execute, and validate both unit and integration tests for distributed applications.

Importance of testing in distributed systems

Testing distributed microservice applications is completely different from testing monolithic applications. Microservices interact with external sources like APIs, message brokers, databases, and run in different environments and languages. Some of the common challenges include:

- **External dependencies**: Each service may depend on others, which makes testing complex.
- **Configuration management**: Difficult to manage environment variables, secrets, and connection strings across services.
- **Infrastructure setup**: Setting up databases, message brokers, and other infrastructure dependencies for running tests.
- **Observability**: Understanding and monitoring failures across service boundaries.

Testing in .NET Aspire

Testing any .NET Aspire distributed application would mainly include multiple layers, such as:

- **Unit testing**: Validating business logic in isolation without any external dependencies.

- **Integration testing**: Validating interactions between different components, such as APIs or databases.

- **End-to-end testing**: Validating the entire distributed application by simulating real user scenarios.

.NET Aspire provides a modern, cloud-ready stack that not only orchestrates distributed systems but also supports robust testing strategies, including unit and integration tests. While Aspire excels at integration and end-to-end testing by spinning up complete applications, it also plays an important supporting role in unit testing.

For the Eshop application, *Figure 7.1* shows how the .NET Aspire testing project starts the app host and other dependency applications before test execution. Here are the detailed steps:

1. The WarehouseAPI.Tests project starts the Eshop App host project.

2. The Eshop.AppHost process starts running.

3. The Eshop.AppHost starts running by invoking and starting all the dependent services like SQL Server, **data API builder (DAB)**, Web API, and React frontend.

4. Once all the dependent services are up and running. The WarehouseAPI.Tests project sends an HTTP request to the frontend application to check for its health.

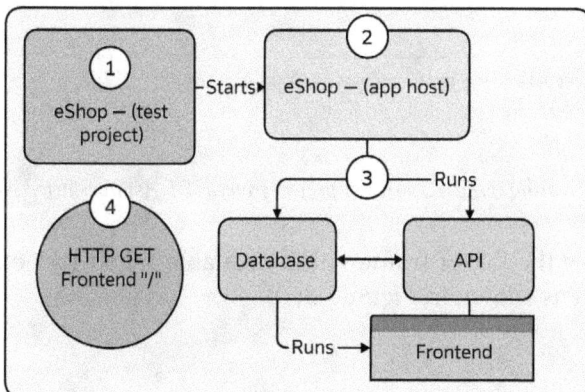

Figure 7.1: *Shows test project setup to run AppHost and its dependencies*

Using the above setup, lets create the test project and write a test method using MSTest framework.

Note: **The main difference between unit testing and .NET Aspire Testing is that if your goal is to test a single method or a component in isolation, write mocks to mock external dependencies to test the functionality, whereas .NET Aspire Testing is used to verify end-to-end functionality of your distributed system.**

Setting up test projects in .NET Aspire

For .NET based services, there are a few popular unit testing frameworks like **xUnit, NUnit,** and **MSTest**. Each framework has its advantages and disadvantages, and based on your project needs, you can pick either one of them. .NET Aspire test project templates are available for all three frameworks.

Figure 7.2 shows how you can add a test project during creation of a .NET Aspire solution with the help of the **.NET Aspire Starter App** template:

Additional information

.NET Aspire Starter App   C#   .NET Aspire   API   Blazor   Cloud   Common   Service   Web   Web API

Framework ⓘ

| .NET 8.0 (Long Term Support) | ▾ |

☑ Configure for HTTPS ⓘ

.NET Aspire version ⓘ

| 9.0 | ▾ |

☐ Use Redis for caching (requires a supported container runtime) ⓘ

Create a test project ⓘ

| None | ▾ |

Figure 7.2: Creating .NET Aspire test project from .NET Aspire Starter App template

You can see the list of frameworks available when you expand the drop down as shown in *Figure 7.3*:

Create a test project ⓘ

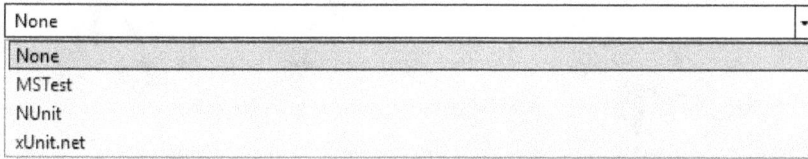

None	▼

None
MSTest
NUnit
xUnit.net

Figure 7.3: *List of popular test frameworks available in the*
.NET Aspire Starter App template

We can also add the test project by right-clicking on the existing solution to add a new project. In the opened dialog, the list of **.NET Aspire Test Project** templates is available as shown in *Figure 7.4*:

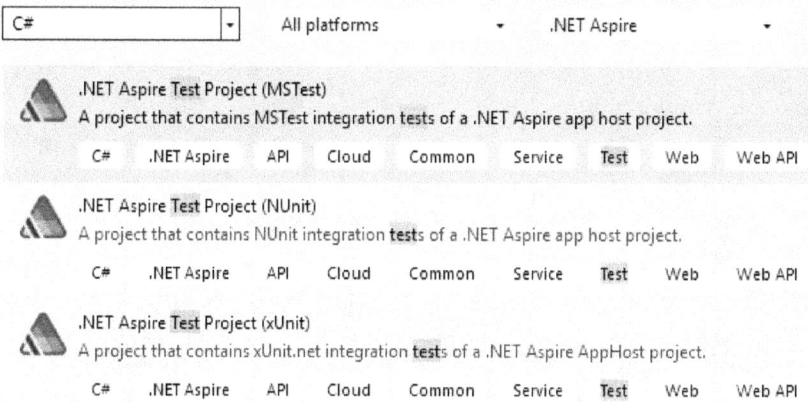

C#	▼	All platforms	▼	.NET Aspire	▼

.NET Aspire Test Project (MSTest)
A project that contains MSTest integration tests of a .NET Aspire app host project.

C#	.NET Aspire	API	Cloud	Common	Service	Test	Web	Web API

.NET Aspire Test Project (NUnit)
A project that contains NUnit integration tests of a .NET Aspire app host project.

C#	.NET Aspire	API	Cloud	Common	Service	Test	Web	Web API

.NET Aspire Test Project (xUnit)
A project that contains xUnit.net integration tests of a .NET Aspire AppHost project.

C#	.NET Aspire	API	Cloud	Common	Service	Test	Web	Web API

Figure 7.4: *List of .NET Aspire Test Project templates for popular test frameworks*

In this chapter, we will use the MSTest as the framework for creating .NET Aspire testing projects.

Select the MSTest template and click **Next** to enter the project name as **WarehouseAPI.Tests** as shown in *Figure 7.5*:

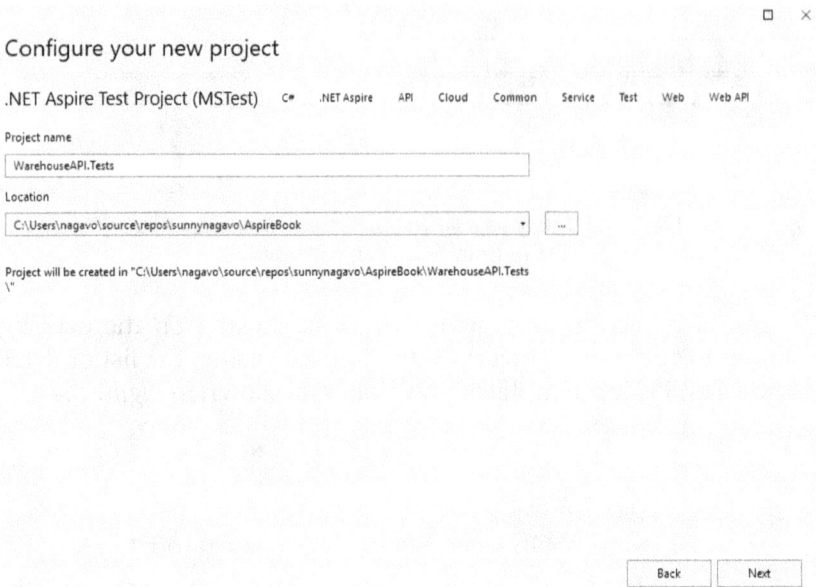

Figure 7.5: *Configure new .NET Aspire Test Project (MSTest)
dialog from Visual Studio IDE*

Select framework as **.NET 9.0 (Standard Term Support)** and click
create, as shown in *Figure 7.6,* to add a new test project to the existing
solution.

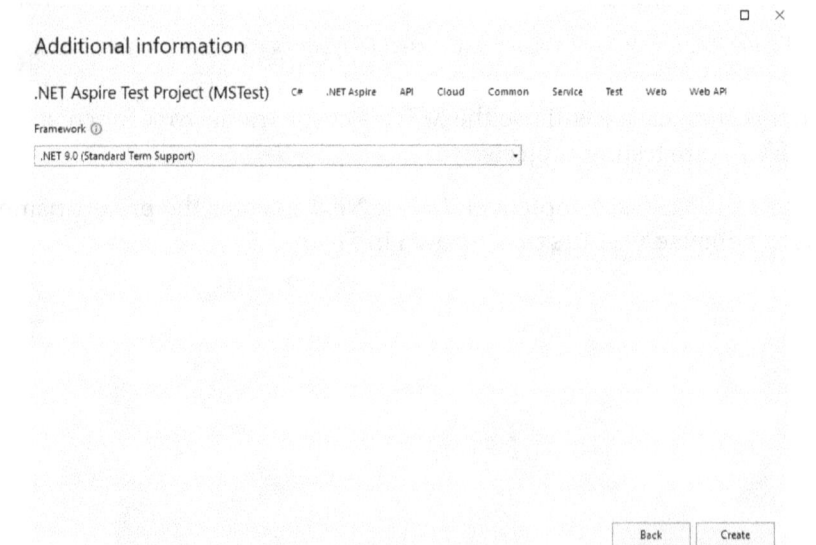

Figure 7.6: *Framework selection dialog when creating a new test project*

Once the test project is created and added to the solution, it will include all the required packages like **Aspire.Hosting.Testing** and MSTest. We also added **Moq** for adding Mocks as shown in *Figure 7.7*.

You can also add a test project to an existing .NET Aspire project using the .NET CLI as shown in the following:

```
dotnet new aspire-mstest
```

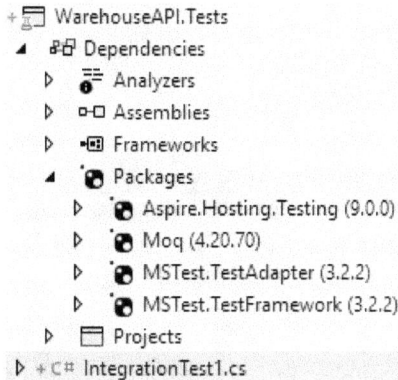

Figure 7.7: Shows a list of packages added by default in the test project

The **WarehouseAPI.Tests** project will have this list of all dependency projects inside the **WarehouseAPI.tests.csproj** file as shown in the following:

```
<ItemGroup>
    <PackageReference Include="MSTest.TestAdapter" />
    <PackageReference Include="MSTest.TestFramework" />
    <PackageReference Include="Moq" />
    <PackageReference Include="Aspire.Hosting.Testing"/>
</ItemGroup>
```

Let us look at brief details about each package reference included in above code.

- **MSTest.TestAdapter**: Allows IDEs to discover and execute MSTest based unit tests in the project

- **MSTest.TestFramework**: It provides core MSTest attributes and assertion methods needed to write and run tests.

- **Moq**: A popular mocking library for .NET.

- **Aspire.Hosting.Testing**: Provides necessary tools and support for testing .NET Aspire applications, including support for in-memory hosting and service orchestration.

Add the .NET Aspire AppHost project as a project reference inside the tests project. Since we use external services, containers, and other projects, we must reference AppHost projects, so that resource resolution happens during the actual unit tests execution:

```
<ItemGroup>
        <ProjectReference Include="..\src\Aspire-
Orchestration\Eshop.AppHost\Eshop.AppHost.csproj" />  </
ItemGroup>
```

To write tests related to WarehouseAPI, you also need to add project references to refer to **WarehouseAPI.csproj**. Right-click on dependencies inside WarehouseAPI.Tests to add project dependencies:

```
<ItemGroup>
        <ProjectReference Include="..\src\WarehouseAPI\
WarehouseAPI.csproj" />  </ItemGroup>
```

Complete **WarehouseAPI.Tests.csproj** will look like the following:

```
<Project Sdk="Microsoft.NET.Sdk">

  <PropertyGroup>
    <TargetFramework>net9.0</TargetFramework>
    <ImplicitUsings>enable</ImplicitUsings>
    <Nullable>enable</Nullable>
    <IsPackable>false</IsPackable>
    <IsTestProject>true</IsTestProject>
    <EnableMSTestRunner>true</EnableMSTestRunner>
    <OutputType>Exe</OutputType>
  </PropertyGroup>

  <ItemGroup>
    <PackageReference Include="MSTest.TestAdapter" />
    <PackageReference Include="MSTest.TestFramework" />
    <PackageReference Include="Aspire.Hosting.Testing" />
  </ItemGroup>

  <ItemGroup>
```

```
    <ProjectReference Include="..\src\Aspire-
Orchestration\Eshop.AppHost\Eshop.AppHost.csproj" />
    <ProjectReference Include="..\src\WarehouseAPI\
WarehouseAPI.csproj" />
  </ItemGroup>

</Project>
```

By default, the **IntegrationTest1.cs** file is added, which contains a single test named **GetWebResourceRootReturnsOkStatusCode** with commented code explaining how to add project references. Update the code with the correct AppHost project, and once modified and uncommented, it will look as shown in the following:

```
using Aspire.Hosting.ApplicationModel;
using Aspire.Hosting.Testing;
using Microsoft.Extensions.DependencyInjection;
using Microsoft.VisualStudio.TestTools.UnitTesting;
using System.Net;

namespace WarehouseAPI.Tests
{
    [TestClass]
    public class IntegrationTest1
    {
        [TestMethod]
        public async Task
GetWebResourceRootReturnsOkStatusCode()
        {
            // Arrange
            var appHost = await
DistributedApplicationTestingBuilder.
CreateAsync<Projects.Eshop_AppHost>();
            appHost.Services.
ConfigureHttpClientDefaults(clientBuilder =>
            {
                clientBuilder.
AddStandardResilienceHandler();
            });
            await using var app = await appHost.
BuildAsync();
            var resourceNotificationService = app.Services.
```

```
GetRequiredService<ResourceNotificationService>();
        await app.StartAsync();

        // Act
        var httpClient = app.
CreateHttpClient("frontend-react-app");
        await resourceNotificationService.
WaitForResourceAsync("frontend-react-app",
KnownResourceStates.Running).WaitAsync(TimeSpan.
FromSeconds(30));
        var response = await httpClient.
GetAsync("/");

        // Assert
        Assert.AreEqual(HttpStatusCode.OK, response.
StatusCode);
    }
  }
}
```

The above test, **GetWebResourceRootReturnsOkStatusCode**, begins with setting up a distributed application host specifically configured for integration tests. Once the application is started, the test waits until the **frontend-react-app** resource is fully running before proceeding. It then sends an HTTP GET Request to the root path of the front-end app and checks if the response status code is **HttpStatusCode.OK** (200) or not.

Unlike unit tests that isolate and mock dependencies, this method tests the application's end-to-end capabilities by creating a test instance of the full distributed application, configuring resilience patterns for HTTP communications, starting all microservices, and then validating that the front-end application is correctly responding to HTTP requests. It also follows the **Arrange-Act-Assert (AAA)** pattern, which we will discuss in the *Unit testing* section.

This integration test provides validation that the application components work together correctly in an ideal environment by giving enough confidence to the developers that production deployments will function as expected.

Introduction to unit testing

Unit Testing is an important piece in the **software development life cycle (SDLC)**, which ensures quality and reliability of software, particularly in microservices architectures where each individual service must work correctly both in isolation and as part of a larger system. In today's world of developing polyglot microservices, where each service is implemented in a different language and framework, unit testing provides the path to validate the core logic of each independent service, regardless of its technology stack. Let us understand the core benefits of unit testing in microservices:

- **Faster feedback**: Developers can quickly iterate on their changes and verify without worrying about other dependent systems.

- **Early identification of issues**: Code bugs / issues are caught early before integration, which reduces debugging efforts.

- **Confidence in refactoring**: Developers can confidently refactor their code without worrying too much about introducing regressions in the code, as unit tests will help us guard core functionality.

- **Faster releases**: With early identification of issues, developers can focus on fixing the issues instead of spending a lot of time debugging. This leads to a boost in productivity and faster release cycles.

Adding unit tests

While .NET Aspire is created mainly for orchestrating and testing distributed systems, it also supports unit testing of individual services. Unit tests in .NET are written in isolation from infrastructure, where we use dependency injection and mocks to avoid external dependencies so that tests are focused on business logic and are faster to run.

Add reference to the Moq NuGet package, which is used for creating mocks:

```
<ItemGroup>
        <PackageReference Include="Moq" />
</ItemGroup>
```

Let us create a unit test for checking the response of **GetWarehouseStatus** to see what the returned responses are when there are some pending orders. The unit tests are written by following the AAA pattern, which is a structured approach to writing clean, readable, and maintainable unit tests:

- **Arrange**: This section ensures creating test objects, setting up data, configuring mocks, and creating preconditions for the test.

- **Act**: This section ensures calling a single method to capture the behavior or result being verified.

- **Assert**: This section verifies actual vs expected results with the help of Assert statements.

While writing unit tests, it is important to note that the name of the unit test method should clearly explain the intent of the method. For simplicity, unit test methods are divided into three parts as shown in the following:

<Name of the method under test>_ <returned response>_<input parameters>

Based on the above unit test method format, the name of the method now becomes **GetWarehouseStatus_ReturnsAvailableItems_ WhenNoPendingOrders**. This is a unit test that focuses on the **GetWarehouseStatus()** method and verifies that when there are no pending orders, the client correctly returns the list of all available warehouse items. This can be validated by making use of Assert statements. The entire code for this method is as shown in the following:

```
[TestMethod]
 public async Task GetWarehouseStatus_
ReturnsAvailableItems_WhenNoPendingOrders()
  {
    // Arrange
    var items = new List<WarehouseItem>
    {
        new(1, "ItemA", 10, DateTime.UtcNow),
        new(2, "ItemB", 5, DateTime.UtcNow)
    };
    var orders = new List<Order>(); // No pending orders
```

```
    var httpClient = CreateMockHttpClient(items,
orders);

    var client = new WarehouseClient(httpClient);

    // Act
    var result = await client.GetWarehouseStatus();

    // Assert
    Assert.AreEqual(2, result.Length);
    Assert.IsTrue(result.Any(i => i.ItemID == 1));
    Assert.IsTrue(result.Any(i => i.ItemID == 2));
}
```

As you can see in the above code, we are using the **Moq** framework to create a mock HTTP handler that intercepts specific URL patterns and returns pre-configured responses. The following is the implementation of the **CreateMockHttpClient** method:

```
private static HttpClient
CreateMockHttpClient(List<WarehouseItem> items,
List<Order> orders)
{
    var handlerMock = new Mock<HttpMessageHandler>();

    handlerMock.Protected()
        .Setup<Task<HttpResponseMessage>>(
            "SendAsync",
            ItExpr.Is<HttpRequestMessage>(req => req.
RequestUri!.ToString().Contains("WarehouseItems")),
            ItExpr.IsAny<CancellationToken>()
        )
        .ReturnsAsync(new HttpResponseMessage
        {
            StatusCode = HttpStatusCode.OK,
            Content = new StringContent(JsonSerializer.
Serialize(new DABResponse<WarehouseItem>(items)))
        });

    handlerMock.Protected()
        .Setup<Task<HttpResponseMessage>>(
            "SendAsync",
```

```
        ItExpr.Is<HttpRequestMessage>(req => req.
RequestUri!.ToString().Contains("Orders")),
        ItExpr.IsAny<CancellationToken>()
    )
    .ReturnsAsync(new HttpResponseMessage
    {
        StatusCode = HttpStatusCode.OK,
        Content = new StringContent(JsonSerializer.
Serialize(new DABResponse<Order>(orders)))
    });

    return new HttpClient(handlerMock.Object)
    {
        BaseAddress = new Uri("http://localhost/")
    };
}
```

By consuming the Mock HTTP client method, we are validating the business logic without the complexity, latency, or instability of actual network communications.

Similarly, we also added another method with the name **GetWarehouseStatus_ReturnsAvailableItems_ ExcludesItemsWithPendingOrders**, as the name implies, we are testing the GetWarehoseStatus API and verifying that when there are pending orders, the client correctly returns the list of all available warehouse items by excluding pending orders. This can be validated by making use of Assert statements. The entire code for this method is as shown in the following:

```
[TestMethod]
public async Task GetWarehouseStatus_
ReturnsAvailableItems_ExcludesItemsWithPendingOrders()
{
    // Arrange
    var items = new List<WarehouseItem>
    {
        new(1, "ItemA", 10, DateTime.UtcNow),
        new(2, "ItemB", 5, DateTime.UtcNow)
    };
    var orders = new List<Order>
    {
```

```
      new(100, "Cust", 1, 1, "Pending", DateTime.
UtcNow, DateTime.UtcNow)
    };

    var httpClient = CreateMockHttpClient(items, orders);

    var client = new WarehouseClient(httpClient);

    // Act
    var result = await client.GetWarehouseStatus();

    // Assert
    Assert.AreEqual(1, result.Length);
    Assert.AreEqual(2, result[0].ItemID);
}
```

After adding these unit tests, the entire contents of the **IntegrationTest1.cs** file will look exactly as shown in the following:

```
using Aspire.Hosting.ApplicationModel;
using Aspire.Hosting.Testing;
using Microsoft.Extensions.DependencyInjection;
using Microsoft.VisualStudio.TestTools.UnitTesting;
using System.Net;
using System.Text.Json;
using Moq;
using Moq.Protected;

namespace WarehouseAPI.Tests
{
    [TestClass]
    public class IntegrationTest1
    {
        [TestMethod]
        public async Task
GetWebResourceRootReturnsOkStatusCode()
        {
            // Arrange
            var appHost = await
DistributedApplicationTestingBuilder.
CreateAsync<Projects.Eshop_AppHost>();
```

```
            appHost.Services.
ConfigureHttpClientDefaults(clientBuilder =>
            {
                clientBuilder.
AddStandardResilienceHandler();
            });
            await using var app = await appHost.
BuildAsync();
            var resourceNotificationService = app.Services.
GetRequiredService<ResourceNotificationService>();
            await app.StartAsync();

            // Act
            var httpClient = app.
CreateHttpClient("frontend-react-app");
            await resourceNotificationService.
WaitForResourceAsync("frontend-react-app",
KnownResourceStates.Running).WaitAsync(TimeSpan.
FromSeconds(30));
            var response = await httpClient.
GetAsync("/");

            // Assert
            Assert.AreEqual(HttpStatusCode.OK, response.
StatusCode);
        }

        [TestMethod]
        public async Task GetWarehouseStatus_
ReturnsAvailableItems_WhenNoPendingOrders()
        {
            // Arrange
            var items = new List<WarehouseItem>
            {
                new(1, "ItemA", 10, DateTime.UtcNow),
                new(2, "ItemB", 5, DateTime.UtcNow)
            };
            var orders = new List<Order>(); // No pending
orders

            var httpClient = CreateMockHttpClient(items,
```

```
orders);

            var client = new WarehouseClient(httpClient);

            // Act
            var result = await client.
GetWarehouseStatus();

            // Assert
            Assert.AreEqual(2, result.Length);
            Assert.IsTrue(result.Any(i => i.ItemID ==
1));
            Assert.IsTrue(result.Any(i => i.ItemID ==
2));
        }

        [TestMethod]
        public async Task GetWarehouseStatus_
ExcludesItemsWithPendingOrders()
            {
            // Arrange
            var items = new List<WarehouseItem>
            {
                new(1, "ItemA", 10, DateTime.UtcNow),
                new(2, "ItemB", 5, DateTime.UtcNow)
            };
            var orders = new List<Order>
            {
                new(100, "Cust", 1, 1, "Pending",
DateTime.UtcNow, DateTime.UtcNow)
            };

            var httpClient = CreateMockHttpClient(items,
orders);

            var client = new WarehouseClient(httpClient);

            // Act
            var result = await client.
GetWarehouseStatus();
```

```
            // Assert
            Assert.AreEqual(1, result.Length);
            Assert.AreEqual(2, result[0].ItemID);
        }

        private static HttpClient
CreateMockHttpClient(List<WarehouseItem> items,
List<Order> orders)
        {
            var handlerMock = new
Mock<HttpMessageHandler>();

            handlerMock.Protected()
                .Setup<Task<HttpResponseMessage>>(
                    "SendAsync",
                    ItExpr.Is<HttpRequestMessage>(req =>
req.RequestUri!.ToString().Contains("WarehouseItems")),
                    ItExpr.IsAny<CancellationToken>()
                )
                .ReturnsAsync(new HttpResponseMessage
                {
                    StatusCode = HttpStatusCode.OK,
                    Content = new
StringContent(JsonSerializer.Serialize(new
DABResponse<WarehouseItem>(items)))
                });

            handlerMock.Protected()
                .Setup<Task<HttpResponseMessage>>(
                    "SendAsync",
                    ItExpr.Is<HttpRequestMessage>(req =>
req.RequestUri!.ToString().Contains("Orders")),
                    ItExpr.IsAny<CancellationToken>()
                )
                .ReturnsAsync(new HttpResponseMessage
                {
                    StatusCode = HttpStatusCode.OK,
                    Content = new
StringContent(JsonSerializer.Serialize(new
DABResponse<Order>(orders)))
                });
```

```
        return new HttpClient(handlerMock.Object)
        {
            BaseAddress = new Uri("http://
localhost/")
        };
    }

    }
}
```

Executing integration or unit tests

Visual Studio provides a seamless experience for running and managing your tests through test explorer. Once you build your test project, all your tests will automatically appear in the **Test Explorer** window.

Click the **Test** tab at the top of Visual Studio and open **Test Explorer**. *Figure 7.8* shows the **Test Explorer** view by displaying all the above methods, which were added inside the **IntegrationTest1.cs** file:

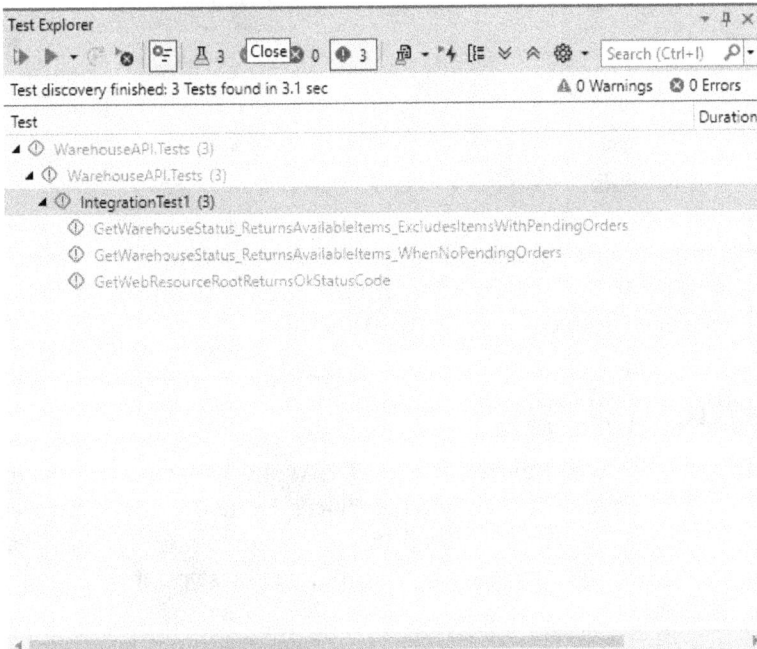

Figure 7.8: Detailed Test Explorer view with list of tests inside IntegrationTest1.cs file

You can run all the tests or select individual tests and run them. You can also debug individual tests to understand their workflow or to debug failures to fix the tests.

Click the run all green button at the top of **Test Explorer** to run all the tests. The **Test Explorer** displays the outcome (**Passed, Failed, Skipped**) for each test. *Figure 7.9* shows the test results of all the tests along with their duration:

Test Explorer		
▶ ▶ ⚲ ⊗ 🔲 3 ⊘ 3 ⊗ 0 ⏸ Close ≫ ≈ ⚙ ▾ Search (Ctrl+I)		
Test run finished: 3 Tests (3 Passed, 0 Failed, 0 Skipped) run in 10.6 sec	⚠ 0 Warnings	⊗ 0 Errors
Test	Duration	Traits
◢ ⊘ WarehouseAPI.Tests (3)	10.1 sec	
◢ ⊘ WarehouseAPI.Tests (3)	10.1 sec	
◢ ⊘ IntegrationTest1 (3)	10.1 sec	
⊘ GetWarehouseStatus_ReturnsAvailableItems_ExcludesItemsWithPendingOrders	2 ms	
⊘ GetWarehouseStatus_ReturnsAvailableItems_WhenNoPendingOrders	100 ms	
⊘ GetWebResourceRootReturnsOkStatusCode	10 sec	

Figure 7.9: Test results by running all tests inside the Integration1.cs file

Integration tests may take longer to execute than unit tests because they spin up the full distributed environment, including all services and resources defined in your AppHost file.

Conclusion

In this chapter, we explored how .NET Aspire is used as a powerful tool for testing distributed microservices by using the Eshop as a practical example. We discussed the importance of unit testing and integration testing, along with how to set up test projects using the MSTest framework by utilizing the .NET Aspire MSTest project template. By leveraging .NET Aspire features such as automated environment setup, checking resource health, and integrated telemetry, developers can write tests to ensure these microservices are reliable and production ready.

In the next chapter, we will lay the foundation for exploring how to build intelligent applications with the help of .NET Aspire and AI integration. We will start with the basics of LLM and orchestrator and show how .NET Aspire, combined with Semantic Kernel and Azure Open AI, can help developers to build AI-driven intelligent distributed systems.

Join our Discord space

Join our Discord workspace for latest updates, offers, tech happenings around the world, new releases, and sessions with the authors:

https://discord.bpbonline.com

CHAPTER 8
.NET Aspire and AI

Introduction

AI has transformed the landscape of building software applications by enabling the creation of intelligent applications that can understand, reason, and interact. However, building intelligent apps is not easy due to the challenges in developing and debugging such applications, which is hard and requires ways to monitor all the traces. This chapter explores how a .NET Aspire addresses these challenges by providing robust support for local development, tracing, and telemetry in AI-driven applications. We will introduce key concepts such as LLMs, orchestrators, agents, and demonstrate with a practical application in integrating AI capabilities using .NET Aspire, Semantic Kernel, and Azure OpenAI.

Structure

In this chapter, we will discuss the following topics:

- Introduction to LLMs and orchestrator

- Using .NET Aspire when building AI applications
- Future trends and upcoming releases

Objectives

By the end of the chapter, you will learn what an LLM orchestrator is and why you should use it. Moreover, we will discuss why .NET Aspire largely improves the developer experience when building intelligent apps.

Introduction to LLMs and orchestrator

Large language models (**LLMs**) are advanced types of AI trained to understand and generate human-like language. The extensive training that built these models allows them to perform a variety of natural language tasks such as answering questions, translating languages, summarizing text, writing code, and even holding conversations. Models like GPT-4o, for instance, can interpret not only individual words but also relationships and patterns that exist across entire sentences.

A core concept behind how an LLM formulates an answer is the context. Context refers to the surrounding information that we provide the LLM to provide an answer to a question. You could open ChatGPT and ask the model to analyze your annual budget trend to identify the major expense categories. GPT would understand your request, but it would not have the correct data to provide you with an answer. We need to improve the context by providing the model with such data.

There are two ways to provide data to an LLM: using the prompt or implementing the **retrieval-augmented generation** (**RAG**) pattern.

Using the prompt implies sending the data along with the request. In the previous example, you could open ChatGPT and ask a question such as *Here is my credit card transaction for the last month. Could you identify the category in which I have spent the most?* and attach to the request a JSON file containing the extracted data from your credit card. You could even do this programmatically, writing your own code that retrieves certain data by attaching the data to the prompt.

However, your intelligent application would only be able to answer questions related to one data source. To make matters worse, the data might require filters before being retrieved. How could you populate those filters based on the user request?

Imagine if the LLM could retrieve knowledge autonomously by calling a function with specific parameters based on user requests. Function calling has revolutionized context management in intelligent app development. Now we can send a request to an LLM via API, appending a list of tools with the parameters needed to invoke them. A tool is a piece of code you wrote. Considering the .NET language, a tool is a method, described by its signature. The signature can be enriched by natural language to help the LLM understand what a certain tool does and how and when to use it.

With function calling, you could think of your request to the LLM as something like a conversation that develops like this:

- Code: The user would like to understand what the expense category she spent the most money on was in the last month, and I have a function that can allow me to retrieve her expense report with a filter by date. The current month is June.

- LLM: Please invoke the function to retrieve the user's expense report. Filter starting from the beginning of June.

- Code: I invoked the function and retrieved the following data: [expense_report_data].

- LLM: Given the user request and the context provided, the answer is [expense_category].

This is a human-like representation of what would happen between your code and the LLM. This communication would instead be in a JSON format, with specific conventions.

This is a significant improvement. However, you currently need to manage everything in your code: wrapping each request with the correct information, handling the LLM response, and determining if it requests a function or provides an answer. This is where the LLM orchestrators become important.

An LLM orchestrator is a system or framework that manages the interaction between LLMs and other components of an application or workflow. Rather than simply sending a single prompt to a model and returning the output, an orchestrator coordinates multi-step, multi-agent, or context-rich processes where the LLM needs to interact with tools, retrieve information, maintain memory, or collaborate with other services to complete a complex task.

Moreover, an LLM orchestrator allows the developer to build agents. An agent is a system that uses an LLM as a reasoning engine to autonomously take actions toward achieving a goal. The two key components of an agent are the system prompt and its tools. The system prompt is a set of instructions that describe what the agent can or cannot do, how it provides answers, and so on.

In this chapter, we will use the Semantic Kernel as an LLM orchestrator. Semantic Kernel is a lightweight, open-source project maintained by Microsoft. One of the key benefits of using Semantic Kernel is that it is polyglot. You can use it in .NET, Python, and Java.

To understand how Semantic Kernel works, we will switch to a simpler example than the expense report analysis one. We will build an agent that can perform basic math operations.

Create a new Console Application and add the required packages using the .NET CLI:

```
dotnet new console
dotnet add package Microsoft.SemanticKernel.Agents.Core
dotnet add package Microsoft.SemanticKernel.Connectors.AzureOpenAI
```

Note: **We will be using Azure OpenAI for this entire chapter. You can refer to both .NET Aspire and Semantic Kernel's official documentation to use other LLM providers (such as OpenAI or Hugging Face).**

Open the project in your editor of choice and create a new class called **MathPlugin.cs**. Add these lines of code:

```
using System;
using System.ComponentModel;
using Microsoft.SemanticKernel;

namespace test;


[Description("Plugin for basic math operations.")]
public class MathPlugin
```

```
{
    [KernelFunction("Add")]
    [Description("Adds two numbers.")]
    public static double Add([Description("first number")]
double a, [Description("second number")]double b)
    {
        return a + b;
    }

    [KernelFunction("Subtract")]
    [Description("Subtracts two numbers.")]
    public static double Subtract([Description("first
number")]double a, [Description("second number")]double
b)
    {
        return a - b;
    }

    [KernelFunction("Multiply")]
    [Description("Multiplies two numbers.")]
    public static double Multiply([Description("first
number")]double a, [Description("second number")]double
b)
    {
        return a * b;
    }

    [KernelFunction("Divide")]
    [Description("Divides two numbers.")]
    public static double Divide([Description("first
number")]double a, [Description("second number")]double
b)
    {
        if (b == 0)
        {
            throw new DivideByZeroException("Cannot
divide by zero.");
        }
        return a / b;
    }
}
```

In this class, we are defining all the tools that our **MathAgent** will be able to use. The code is everything you would expect from a basic .NET class that provides methods to perform math operations. There are two main differences: every method has a **KernelFunction**, and every method and parameter has a **Description** attribute:

- The **KernelFunction** attributes help the Semantic Kernel identify available plugins using reflection.

- The **Description** attributes allow Semantic Kernel to enrich every function and parameter with a human-readable description that will help the LLM in its decision process.

Now that we have the tools, it is time to write the agent itself. In the **Program.cs** class add the following lines:

```
using Microsoft.SemanticKernel;
using Microsoft.SemanticKernel.Agents;
using Microsoft.SemanticKernel.ChatCompletion;
using Microsoft.SemanticKernel.Connectors.OpenAI;
using test;

// Line 7 to 12
IKernelBuilder kernelBuilder = Kernel.CreateBuilder();
var kernel = kernelBuilder.AddAzureOpenAIChatCompletion(
    deploymentName: "YOUR_DEPLOYMNET_NAME",
    apiKey: "YOUR_API_KEY",
    endpoint: "https://YOUR_ENDPOINT.openai.azure.com/"
).Build();

// Line 14 to 19
var _settings = new OpenAIPromptExecutionSettings()
{
    ToolCallBehavior = ToolCallBehavior.
AutoInvokeKernelFunctions,
    Temperature = 0.1,
    MaxTokens = 500,
};

//Line 20 to 27
ChatCompletionAgent mathAgent =
    new()
```

```
    {
        Name = "MathAgent",
        Instructions = "You are a helpful assistant.
Answer the user's questions to the best of your ability
using your tools.",
        Kernel = kernel,
        Arguments = new(_settings)
    };

// Line 28
mathAgent.Kernel.Plugins.AddFromType<MathPlugin>();

ChatHistory chat = [];

chat.Add(new ChatMessageContent(AuthorRole.User, "What is
5 times 3?"));

await foreach (ChatMessageContent response in mathAgent.
InvokeAsync(chat))
{
    Console.WriteLine(response);
}
```

From *lines 7* to *12,* we are building the Kernel itself, providing it with a chat completion model.

From *lines 14* to *19,* we are defining the behavior we want the agent to use. Besides the temperature and maximum number of tokens the LLM should use to generate the response, it should auto-invoke its functions when needed.

From *lines 20* to *27,* we are defining the agent. There are many types of agents available in Semantic Kernel, but in this scenario, we are using the simple **ChatCompletionAgent**. That is, an agent that uses chat completion APIs to provide an answer. Here we also define the system prompt. It can be very complicated to write a correct system prompt for complex agents, and it is usually stored in a separate file because it can be articulated in many lines. In our scenario, we only need one very simple line.

On *line 28,* we use a single line of code to let Semantic Kernel add all the available plugins in the **MathPlugin** class to the **MathAgent**.

The remaining lines of code show a very simple way to use our agent: we add the hardcoded user request and let the agent invoke the chat completion APIs on the **ChatHistory** that we have created.

If you set a breakpoint on *line 28* of the **MathPlugin** class and run this program in debug mode, you should see the code hitting the endpoint, and the parameters **a** and **b** are correctly populated with the values **5** and **3**.

Developers need to understand what occurs during the interaction between the agent and the LLM. When issues arise, developers should comprehend the decisions made by the LLM. If the outcome appears satisfactory but there is uncertainty about whether the tool was utilized or if the response is based solely on the model's training data, steps should be taken to clarify this.

This is why we need .NET Aspire, even when we are developing intelligent applications.

Using .NET Aspire when building AI applications

As shown in the previous paragraph, the conversation between our code and the LLM is at the center of every intelligent application. But to make sure everything is working correctly, or to solve issues when nothing is working as expected, we need observability.

Semantic Kernel is instrumented with OpenTelemetry. Adding .NET Aspire is the perfect way to see in our local environment all the traces coming from the agent, allowing us to analyze every step of the orchestration process.

Start by creating an empty Aspire project and a .NET minimal API project:

```
dotnet new aspire
dotnet new web -o SemanticKernelAgent
```

Add the reference to the **ServiceDefaults** project in the **SemanticKernelAgent** project, and the required packages:

```
cd SemanticKernelAgent
dotnet add package Microsoft.AspNetCore.OpenApi
dotnet add package Aspire.Azure.AI.OpenAI --prerelease
```

```
dotnet add package Microsoft.SemanticKernel
dotnet add package Microsoft.SemanticKernel.Agents.Core
dotnet add package Microsoft.SemanticKernel.Connectors.
AzureOpenAI
dotnet add package System.Text.Json
```

Let us look at the details each package brings in.

- **Microsoft.AspNetCore.OpenApi**: This package is a great option for generating OpenAPI (Swagger) documents for ASP.NET Core minimal APIs or controller-based APIs. It allows you to document APIs easily and discover more about them.

- **Aspire.Azure.AI.OpenAI**: This package enables .NET Aspire-based applications to interface with the Azure OpenAI Service or OpenAI's API. In addition, it allows developers to configure and interface securely with OpenAI models in .NET applications without altering the core application.

- **Microsoft.SemanticKernel**: A lightweight SDK that allows for integration of AI LLMs from .NET applications with prompt engineering capabilities, semantic functions, and advanced AI workflows.

- **Microsoft.SemanticKernel.Agents.Core**: Provides primary agentic capabilities for the Semantic Kernel SDK. It will allow the orchestration of AI agents and the utilization of complex multi-step workflows for elaboration with LLMs.

- **Microsoft.SemanticKernel.Connectors.AzureOpenAI**: Provides connectors/extensions for the Semantic Kernel to the Azure OpenAI platform, supporting chat completion, embedding, and DALL-E image generation clients.

- **System.Text.Json**: High-performance JSON serialization and deserialization APIs for .NET that will allow you to keep it simple with processing JSON data with UTF-8 encoding.

Create a folder named **Plugins** and add the **MathPlugin** class as shown in the following:

```
using System;
using System.ComponentModel;
using Microsoft.SemanticKernel;
```

```
namespace SemanticKernelAgent.Plugins;

[Description("Plugin for basic math operations.")]
public class MathPlugin
{
    [KernelFunction("Add")]
    [Description("Adds two numbers.")]
    public static double Add([Description("first number")]
double a, [Description("second number")]double b)
    {
        return a + b;
    }

    [KernelFunction("Subtract")]
    [Description("Subtracts two numbers.")]
    public static double Subtract([Description("first
number")]double a, [Description("second number")]double
b)
    {
        return a - b;
    }

    [KernelFunction("Multiply")]
    [Description("Multiplies two numbers.")]
    public static double Multiply([Description("first
number")]double a, [Description("second number")]double
b)
    {
        return a * b;
    }

    [KernelFunction("Divide")]
    [Description("Divides two numbers.")]
    public static double Divide([Description("first
number")]double a, [Description("second number")]double
b)
    {
        if (b == 0)
        {
            throw new DivideByZeroException("Cannot
```

```
divide by zero.");
        }
        return a / b;
    }
}
```

This is the same **MathPlugin** class we have used in the console app example.

Now, replace everything in the **Program.cs** file with the code as shown in the following:

```
using System.Text.Json;
using Microsoft.AspNetCore.Mvc;
using Microsoft.SemanticKernel;
using Microsoft.SemanticKernel.Agents;
using Microsoft.SemanticKernel.ChatCompletion;
using Microsoft.SemanticKernel.Connectors.OpenAI;
using SemanticKernelAgent.Plugins;


var builder = WebApplication.CreateBuilder(args);

AppContext.SetSwitch("Microsoft.SemanticKernel.
Experimental.GenAI.EnableOTelDiagnosticsSensitive",
true);

builder.AddServiceDefaults();
builder.AddAzureOpenAIClient("azureOpenAI");
builder.Services.AddOpenApi();
builder.Services.AddSingleton<MathPlugin>();
builder.Services.AddKernel().AddAzureOpenAIChatCompletion
("gpt-4o");
builder.Services.AddSingleton(builder =>
{
    var _settings = new OpenAIPromptExecutionSettings()
    {
        ToolCallBehavior = ToolCallBehavior.
AutoInvokeKernelFunctions,
        Temperature = 0.1,
        MaxTokens = 500,
    };
```

```
    var agent = new ChatCompletionAgent
    {
        Name = "MathAgent",
        Instructions = "You are a helpful assistant.
Answer the user's questions to the best of your ability
using your tools.",
        Kernel = builder.GetRequiredService<Kernel>(),
        Arguments = new(_settings)
    };
    agent.Kernel.Plugins.AddFromObject(builder.
GetRequiredService<MathPlugin>());

    return agent;
});

var app = builder.Build();

// Configure the HTTP request pipeline.
if (app.Environment.IsDevelopment())
{
    app.MapOpenApi();
}

app.MapPost("/agent/chat/stream", async
(ChatCompletionAgent agent, HttpResponse response,
[FromBody]string request) =>
{
    var history = new ChatHistory();
    history.AddUserMessage(request);

    var agentThread = new ChatHistoryAgentThread();

    response.Headers.Append("Content-Type", "application/
jsonl");
    await foreach(var delta in agent.
InvokeStreamingAsync(history, agentThread))
    {
        await response.WriteAsync($"{JsonSerializer.
Serialize(new { Content = delta.Message.Content
})}\r\n");
        await response.Body.FlushAsync();
```

```
        }
})
.WithName("ChatStreamAgent");

app.MapDefaultEndpoints();

app.Run();
```

To enable the collection of traces from Semantic Kernel, we also need to update the code of the **ConfigureOpenTelemetry** method in the **Extensions.cs** file in the **ServiceDefaults** project:

```
public static TBuilder
ConfigureOpenTelemetry<TBuilder>(this TBuilder builder)
where TBuilder : IHostApplicationBuilder
    {
        if(builder.
Configuration["ConnectionStrings:azureOpenAI"] is not null)
            builder.Logging.AddTraceSource("Microsoft.
SemanticKernel");

        builder.Logging.AddOpenTelemetry(logging =>
        {
            logging.IncludeFormattedMessage = true;
            logging.IncludeScopes = true;
        });

        builder.Services.AddOpenTelemetry()
            .WithMetrics(metrics =>
            {
                metrics.AddAspNetCoreInstrumentation()
                    .AddHttpClientInstrumentation()
                    .AddRuntimeInstrumentation();

                if(builder.
Configuration["ConnectionStrings:azureOpenAI"] is not
null)
                    metrics.AddMeter("Microsoft.
SemanticKernel*");
            })
            .WithTracing(tracing =>
            {
```

```
                tracing.AddSource(builder.Environment.
ApplicationName)
                    .AddAspNetCoreInstrumentation(tracing
=>
                    // Exclude health check requests
from tracing
                    tracing.Filter = context =>
                        !context.Request.Path.
StartsWithSegments(HealthEndpointPath)
                            && !context.Request.Path.
StartsWithSegments(AlivenessEndpointPath)
                        )
                    // Uncomment the following line to
enable gRPC instrumentation (requires the OpenTelemetry.
Instrumentation.GrpcNetClient package)
                    //.AddGrpcClientInstrumentation()
                    .AddHttpClientInstrumentation();

            if(builder.
Configuration["ConnectionStrings:azureOpenAI"] is not
null)
                tracing.AddSource("Microsoft.
SemanticKernel*");
            });

        builder.AddOpenTelemetryExporters();

        return builder;
    }
```

Now, every application that has a connection string named **azureOpenAI** will add **Microsoft.SemanticKernel** as a telemetry source.

Now we need to tie everything up with Aspire. Add a connection string in the app settings of the AppHost project using this format:

```
"ConnectionStrings": {
    "azureOpenAI": "Endpoint=https://<YOUR_ENDPOINT>.
openai.azure.com/;Key=<YOUR_KEY>;"
}
```

Replace the content of the **Program.cs** of the AppHost project with the following code:

```
var builder = DistributedApplication.CreateBuilder(args);

var openai = builder.AddConnectionString("azureOpenAI");

builder.AddProject<Projects.SemanticKernelAgent>("agent")
    .WithReference(openai);

builder.Build().Run();
```

Running everything, you can try invoking your API by sending a request such as:

<ENDPOINT>/agent/chat/stream?request=What is 5 times 3?

Now we can use Aspire to see what is going on. *Figure 8.1* shows what the trace will look like:

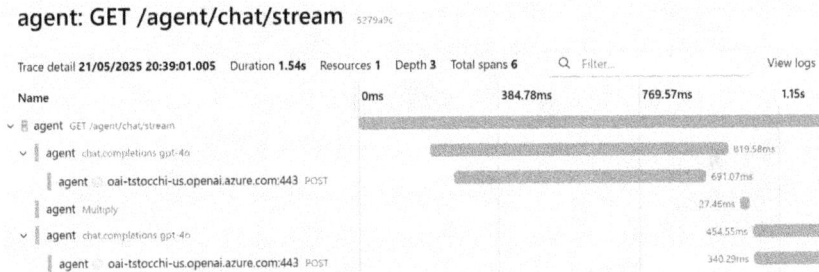

Figure 8.1: Detailed trace of a web API invocation

It is divided into three sections:

- An LLM invocation
- A method execution
- Another LLM invocation

Having enabled the **OTelDiagnosticsSensitive** flag as shown below from the SemanticKernelAgent **Program.cs**:

AppContext.SetSwitch("Microsoft.SemanticKernel. Experimental.GenAI.EnableOTelDiagnosticsSensitive",true);

In the event section of the first LLM invocation, we can see in the following figure what the agent told the LLM and the reply it received:

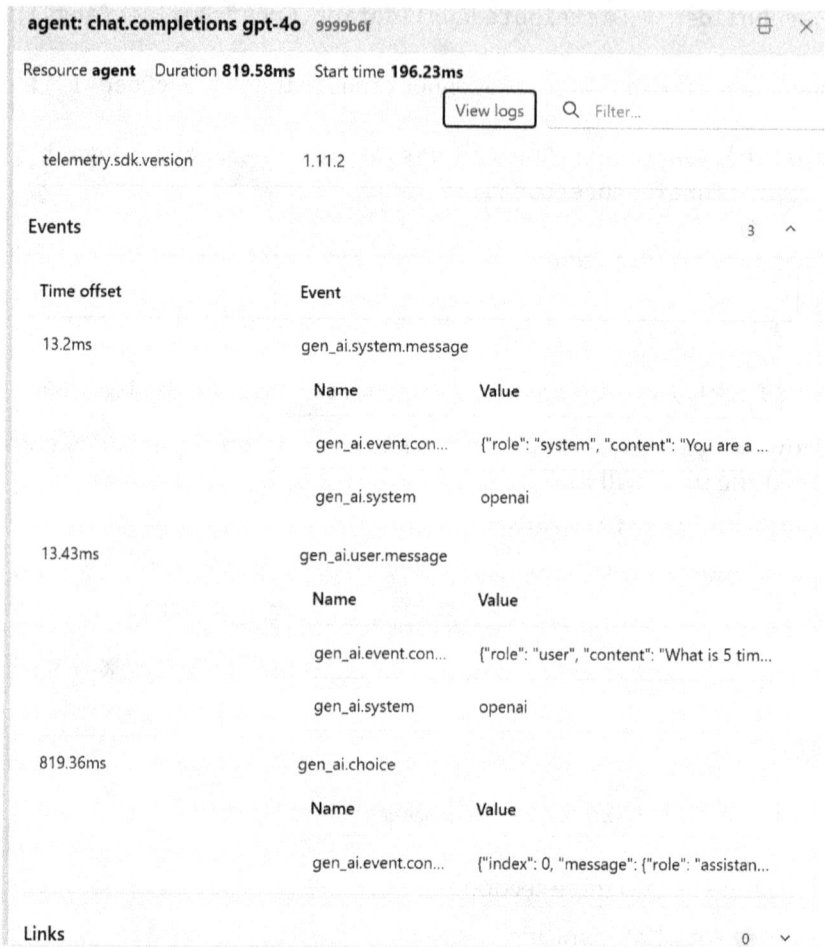

agent: chat.completions gpt-4o 9999b6f   ⊟ ✕

Resource **agent**   Duration **819.58ms**   Start time **196.23ms**

[View logs]   🔍 Filter...

telemetry.sdk.version   1.11.2

Events   3   ᐱ

Time offset	Event
13.2ms	gen_ai.system.message

Name	Value
gen_ai.event.con...	{"role": "system", "content": "You are a ...
gen_ai.system	openai

Time offset	Event
13.43ms	gen_ai.user.message

Name	Value
gen_ai.event.con...	{"role": "user", "content": "What is 5 tim...
gen_ai.system	openai

Time offset	Event
819.36ms	gen_ai.choice

Name	Value
gen_ai.event.con...	{"index": 0, "message": {"role": "assistan...

Links   0   ᐯ

Figure 8.2: The view of a single OpenTelemetry Activity emitted by Semantic Kernel

The **gen_ai.system.message** is the system prompt, basically the instructions we have given the agent. The **gen_ai.user.message** represents the user request and the **gen_ai.choice** is the LLM response. Refer to the following figure:

🔁 gen_ai.event.content

Select format ∨   ✕

```
1   {
2     "index": 0,
3     "message": {
4       "role": "assistant",
5       "content": "",
6       "tool_calls": [
7         {
8           "id": "call_QWqctfqUps6IYNPOddUXxhTw",
9           "function": {
10            "arguments": {
11              "a": "5",
12              "b": "3"
13            },
14            "name": "Multiply"
15          },
16          "type": "function"
17        }
18      ]
```

🗐 Copy to clipboard

Figure 8.3: The expanded view of a single event showing the LLM response

The LLM is telling the agent which function to call and the values to put in the parameters. Since we are using Semantic Kernel, we do not need to parse this response via code and invoke the method ourselves. If you look at the details of the second section of this trace, you will see that the multiply method has been invoked by the Semantic Kernel. Refer to the following figure:

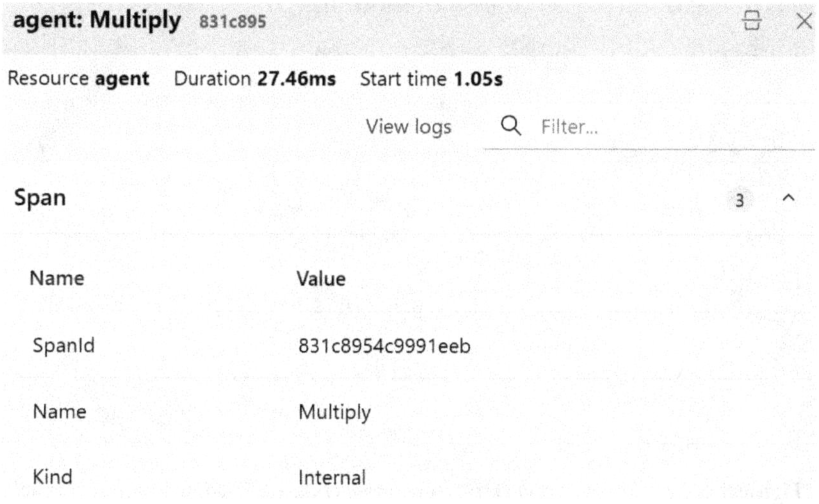

agent: Multiply 831c895   🖥 ✕

Resource **agent**   Duration **27.46ms**   Start time **1.05s**

View logs   🔍 Filter...

Span   3 ∧

Name	Value
SpanId	831c8954c9991eeb
Name	Multiply
Kind	Internal

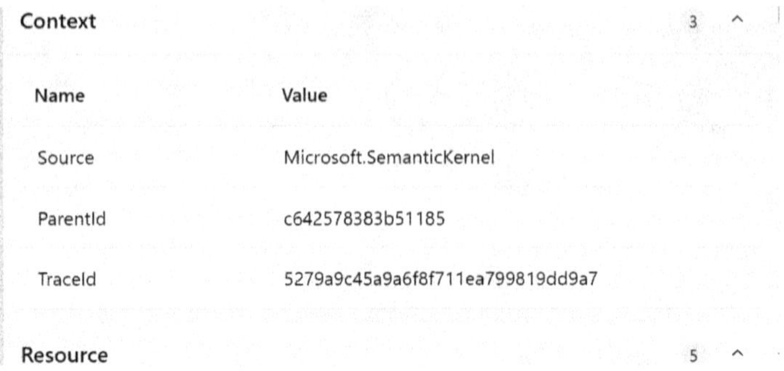

Context		3 ^

Name	Value
Source	Microsoft.SemanticKernel
ParentId	c642578383b51185
TraceId	5279a9c45a9a6f8f711ea799819dd9a7

Resource   5 ^

Figure 8.4: The detailed view of the function calling activity emitted by the Semantic Kernel

In the last section of the trace we see another request to the LLM, where the agent is proving everything it has sent before plus the previous assistant response model APIs are stateless, so the agent needs to provide the entire conversation history with the LLM so far, and the `gen_ai.tool.message` that contains the tool result. Refer to the following figure:

agent: chat.completions gpt-4o ce3cfba   ⊟ ✕

Resource **agent**   Duration **454.55ms**   Start time **1.08s**

View logs   🔍 Filter...

	gen_ai.event...	{"role": "Assistant", "content": "...
	gen_ai.system	openai

80.1µs   gen_ai.tool.message

Name	Value
gen_ai.event...	{"role": "tool", "content": "15"}
gen_ai.system	openai

454.54ms   gen_ai.choice

Name	Value
gen_ai.event...	{"index": 0, "message": {"role": ...

Links   0 ˅

Backlinks   0 ˅

Figure 8.5: The view of a single OpenTelemetry activity emitted by Semantic Kernel

The LLM will review the entire request considering: the system prompt, the user request, the fact that an assistant has requested a tool invocation, and that the tool has returned 15 as a result. The generated response, therefore, is shown in the following figure:

📟 gen_ai.event.content   Select format ∨   ✕

```
1  {
2    "index": 0,
3    "message": {
4      "role": "assistant",
5      "content": "5 times 3 is 15."
6    },
7    "tool_calls": [],
8    "finish_reason": null
9  }
```

🗍 Copy to clipboard

Figure 8.6: The expanded view of a single event showing the LLM response

This is a simple example of what an intelligent application can do. However, it proves that even in such simple scenarios, having the ability to observe our application with modern tools is fundamental to achieving our goal.

Future trends and upcoming releases

The rate at which the .NET Aspire team is releasing its versions is unbelievable. The Microsoft's .NET Aspire team released a new update, which is .NET Aspire 9.3.0, announced as part of Microsoft Build 2025, and it contains several exciting features we thought should be covered in this final section.

To update to the latest version, you can do it via the NuGet Package Manager user interface or through the NuGet Package Manager console. In our solution, we have project-level variables that are used for updating the versions.

Open **Directory.Build.Props** file inside the project folder, to update the **AspireVersion** as shown in the following. The Aspire Community Toolkit version is updated to the latest beta at the time of this book.

```
<Project>
    <!-- See https://aka.ms/dotnet/msbuild/customize for
more details on customizing your build -->
```

```
<PropertyGroup>
  <TargetFramework>net8.0</TargetFramework>
  <LangVersion>latest</LangVersion>

  <ImplicitUsings>enable</ImplicitUsings>
  <Nullable>enable</Nullable>

  <AspireVersion>9.3.0</AspireVersion>
  <CommunityToolkitAspireVersion>9.3.0</
CommunityToolkitAspireVersion>
  <CommunityToolkitAspireVersionBeta>9.4.1-beta.291</
CommunityToolkitAspireVersionBeta>
  <AspNetCoreVersion>8.0.7</AspNetCoreVersion>
  <OpenTelemetryVersion>1.9.0</OpenTelemetryVersion>

  <IsPackable>false</IsPackable>
</PropertyGroup>
</Project>
```

After upgrading and restoring new packages, when you run the Aspire project. Now you will see the dashboard with the GitHub Copilot chat button on the top right pane as shown in *Figure 8.7*:

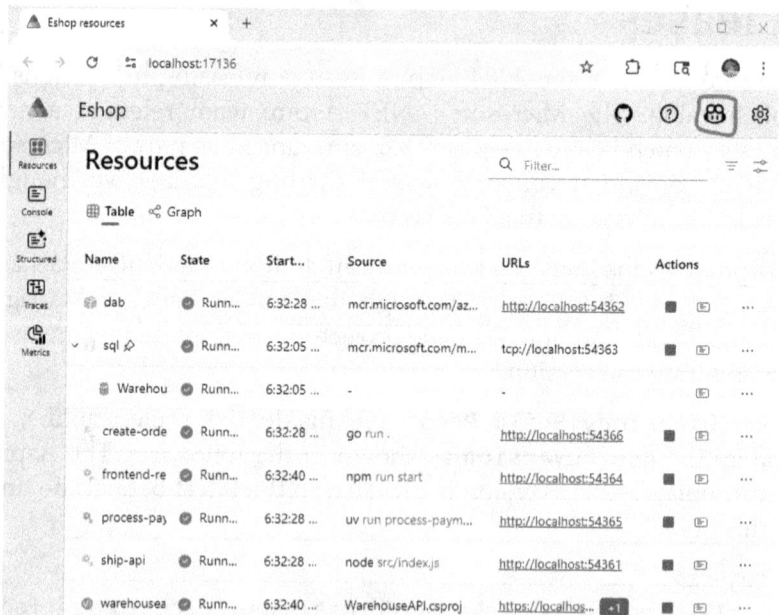

Figure 8.7: Displaying the GitHub Copilot icon on the top-right side

You can also open GitHub Copilot by selecting the three dots on every resource on the dashboard and clicking on the **Actions** button to display the **Ask GitHub Copilot** option as shown in *Figure 8.8:*

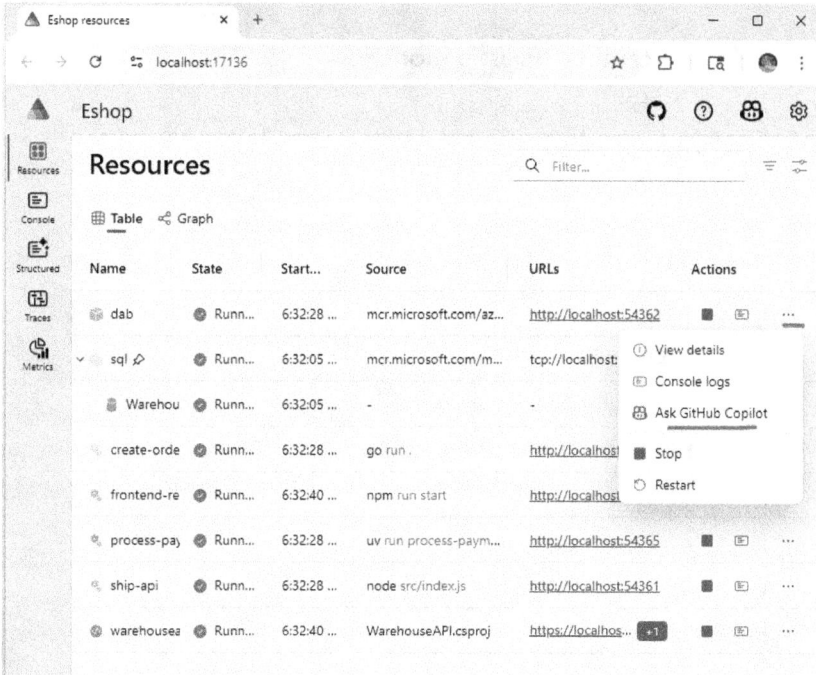

Figure 8.8: Display of the Ask GitHub Copilot option via the Actions button

By clicking on the **Ask GitHub Copilot**, it will open a right-side pane, and you can ask detailed questions about a particular resource, like running state and health, architecture-related details, and whether it is healthy or not. *Figure 8.9* shows the detailed analysis of the **dab** resource inside the **GitHub Copilot chat** window:

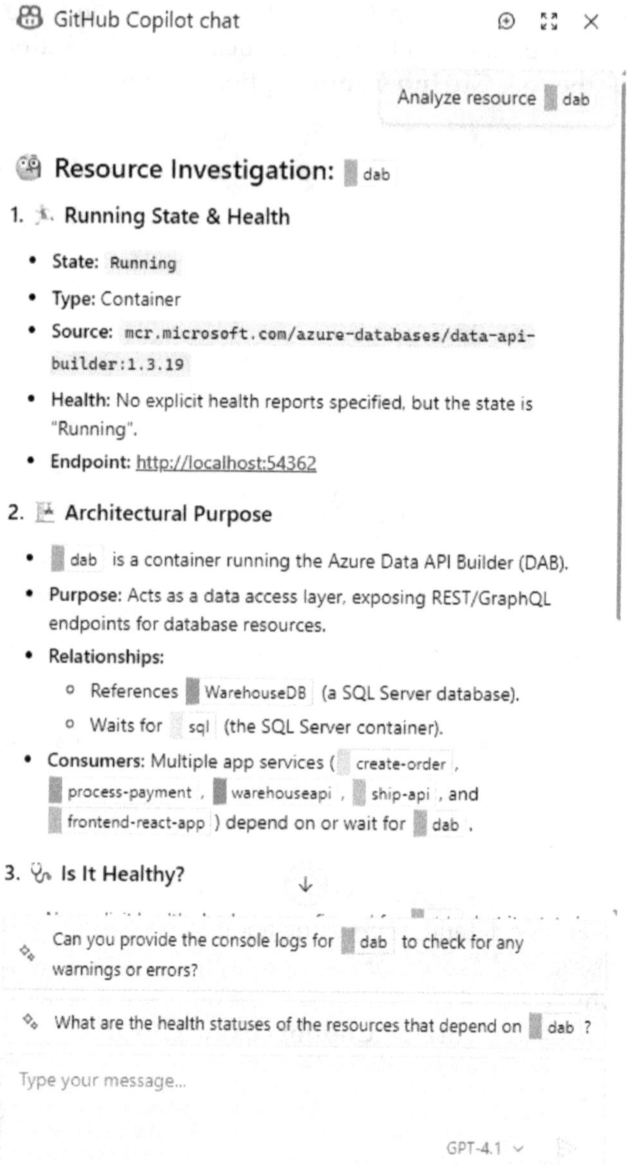

Figure 8.9: Detailed analysis of the dab resource from the GitHub Copilot

We can also analyze distributed traces and logs and ask relevant questions to GitHub Copilot, which can read complete logs to give us the right details. To simulate, a **500 Internal Server Error** is thrown from dab, and let us ask **GitHub Copilot chat** by clicking on traces to analyze a specific trace. *Figure 8.10* shows how GitHub

Copilot analyzes a particular distributed trace and provides complete details about the trace overview, along with error details, including **Root Cause,** log highlights, exceptions thrown, and next steps on how to investigate the error thrown from the server side.

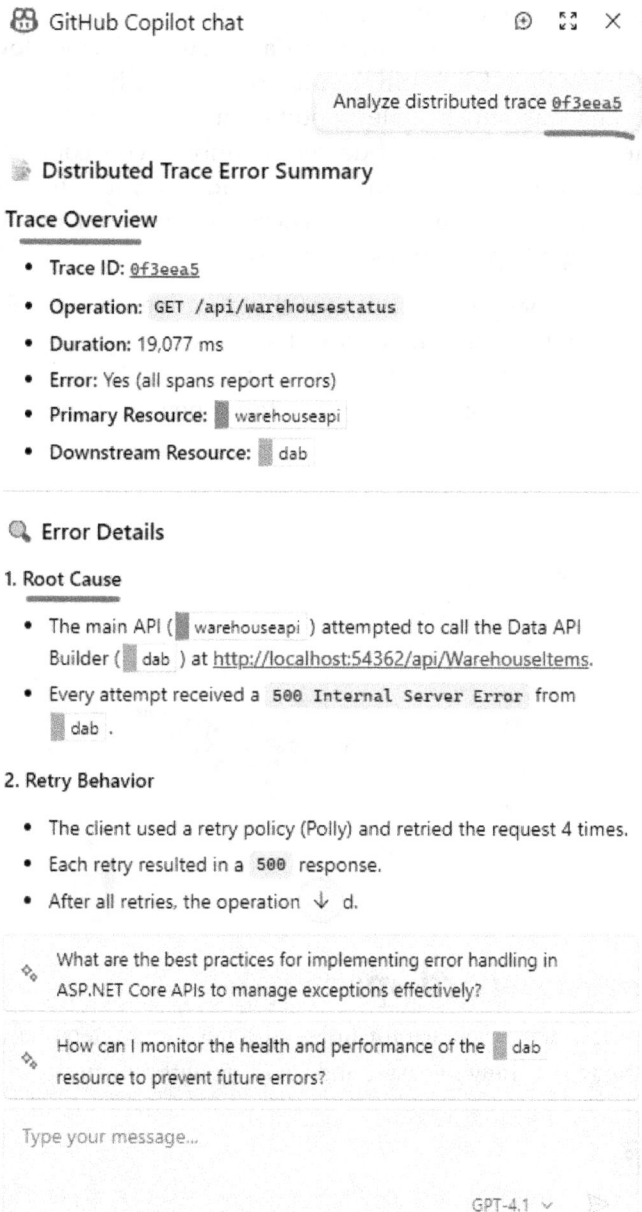

GitHub Copilot chat

Analyze distributed trace 0f3eea5

Distributed Trace Error Summary

Trace Overview

- Trace ID: 0f3eea5
- Operation: GET /api/warehousestatus
- Duration: 19,077 ms
- Error: Yes (all spans report errors)
- Primary Resource: warehouseapi
- Downstream Resource: dab

Error Details

1. Root Cause

- The main API (warehouseapi) attempted to call the Data API Builder (dab) at http://localhost:54362/api/WarehouseItems.
- Every attempt received a 500 Internal Server Error from dab .

2. Retry Behavior

- The client used a retry policy (Polly) and retried the request 4 times.
- Each retry resulted in a 500 response.
- After all retries, the operation ↓ d.

What are the best practices for implementing error handling in ASP.NET Core APIs to manage exceptions effectively?

How can I monitor the health and performance of the dab resource to prevent future errors?

Type your message...

GPT-4.1 ∨

Figure 8.10: A detailed analysis of a particular distributed trace from GitHub Copilot

Conclusion

In this chapter, we have seen what an LLM orchestrator is and the challenges a developer can face when building an LLM-infused application. We have also seen how to overcome those challenges using .NET Aspire and telemetry to analyze LLM workflows. The latest features in .NET Aspire to integrate with GitHub Copilot for resource analysis and troubleshooting, empowering developers to build, debug, and release AI-driven solutions with confidence. As .NET aspire continues to evolve at a rapid pace, it is important to watch for the latest releases to harness the power of building AI-driven intelligent applications.

.NET Aspire is changing the future of cloud-native .NET development by providing powerful tools for distributed microservices. With support from Microsoft and the community, Aspire is here to stay and is committed to innovating by adding new functionality in the upcoming releases.

Join our Discord space

Join our Discord workspace for latest updates, offers, tech happenings around the world, new releases, and sessions with the authors:

https://discord.bpbonline.com

Index

A

AddAspNetCoreInstrumenta-
tion 82
AddGolangApp 67
AddHttpClientInstrumentation
83
AddOpenTelemetryExporters
method 10, 84, 85
AddRuntimeInstrumentation
83
AddServiceDefaults 10
AppHost 27
ApplicationBuilder 10
application programming
interface
(API) 9
appsettings.json file 13

Arrange-Act-Assert (AAA)
pattern 164
Aspire.Hosting.Testing 162
Azure Container App 101
Azure Developer CLI (azd) 93,
94
advanced features 130-132
benefits 94-96
configuring 96-100
for Eshop application development 119, 125-130
installing 96
use case 101-119
using, with .NET Aspire 101-
119
Azure Resource Manager
(ARM) 95
azure.yaml file 102

B
Bicep 95

C
ChatCompletionAgent 183
ChatHistory 184
Client resources 24
Cloud Native Computing
    Foundation
    (CNCF) 78
code structure, warehouse
    backend API
  appsettings.json file 38
  dab-config.json file 33, 35
  launchsettings.json file 37, 38
  Program.cs file 39, 40
  Warehouseclient.cs 35-37
ConfigureOpenTelemetry
    method 10, 82
context 178
CRUD operations 28

D
DABResponse 35
Dapr 135, 136
  adding, to remaining APIs
    144-151
  building blocks 137, 138
  configuring, for Azure de-
    ployment 151, 152
  importance 138, 139
  integrating, with .NET Aspire
    139-141
  using, in Golang 143
  using, in .NET Aspire 141-143
Data API builder 21, 28, 29
  adding, to AppHost 40-47
Data Transfer Objects
    (DTO) 35

development environment
  setting up 22, 23
Directory.Build.Props file 195
DistributedApplication builder
    64
distributed applications
  challenges 2

E
Eshop application
  architecture 18-20
  developing, with azd 119-130
  running, from Visual Studio
    47, 48
external services
  orchestrating, with .NET
    Aspire 64-73

F
FirstApp.ApiService 9
FirstApp.AppHost project 14
FirstApp.ServiceDefaults 9
FirstApp.Web 9

G
GetWarehouseStatus() method
    166
GitHub Copilot 197
GrpcClientInstrumentation 10

H
health checks
  implementing, in .NET Aspire
    85, 86
Hosting resources 24
HttpClientInstrumentation 10
.http files
  using in Visual Studio,
      for API validation 48, 49

I

infrastructure as code (IaC) 95
instrumentation 80
integration tests
  executing 173, 174

L

large language models (LLMs)
    178, 179
LF (Line Feed) termination
    character 43
LLM orchestrator 179-184

M

MapDefaultEndoints 11
Massachusetts Institute of
    Technology (MIT) 28
MathAgent 183
MathPlugin class 183, 184
microservices
  implementation 54-63
monitoring
  benefits 76, 77
  in cloud-native applications
    76
Moq 161
MSTest 158
MSTest.TestAdapter 161
MSTest.TestFramework 161

N

.NET 9.0 160
.NET Aspire 1, 4-6
  future trends 195-199
  health checks 85, 86
  history 2-4
  templates 6, 7
  testing 156, 157
  upcoming releases 195-199

using, when building AI
    applications 184-195
.NET Aspire applications
  instrumenting, with
    OpenTelemetry 80
.NET Aspire Community
    Toolkit 47
.NET Aspire integrations 24-28
  benefits 23
.NET Aspire starter app 7
  creating, with CLI 7
  creating, with Visual Studio
    2022 7-18
.NET Aspire Starter App
    template 158
.NET Aspire Test Project
    templates 159
NUnit 158

O

observability 77, 78
OpenTelemetry 78
  benefits 79
  components 79, 80
  instrumentation 80
  logs 78
  metrics 78
  .NET Aspire application,
    instrumenting with 80
  setting up, in Warehouse API
    project 80-85
  traces 78
OpenTelemetry Line Protocol
    (OTLP) 80

P

polyglot microservices
    architecture
  advantages 53

Process Payment API 145
.PusblishAsDockerfile() 125
publisher/subscriber (pub/
    sub) messaging 136

R
Redis cache 25
retrieval-augmented generation
    (RAG) pattern 178

S
Semantic Kernel 184
service integrations 54
software development life cycle
    (SDLC) 165

T
Telemetry
  analyzing 87-90
  visualizing 87-90
templates 6
Test Explorer 173
testing
  in distributed microservice
      applications 156
  in .NET Aspire 156, 157
test projects
  setting up, in .NET Aspire
      158-164

U
unit testing 165
  benefits 165
unit tests
  adding 165-169
  executing 173, 174

V
Visual Studio 2022
  for creating .NET Aspire start-
      er app 7-17
  for creating warehouse back-
      end API 30-33

W
WaitFor method 15
WarehouseAPI project
  OpenTelemetry, setting up
      80-83
WarehouseAPI.Tests project
    161
warehouse backend API
  code structure 33
  creating 29
  creating, with CLI 29
  creating, with Visual Studio
      2022 30-33
WebApplication object 11
WithArgs(allArgs) method 70
WithOtlpExporter() method 73

X
xUnit 158